My Journey from Disability and Disaster
to Possibility and Empowerment

BEYOND CALAMITY

A SOUTH SUDANESE REFUGEE'S STORY

I0192313

ESTHER SIMBI

ISBN: 978-1-925846-49-2
Published by Vivid Publishing
A division of Fontaine Publishing Group
P.O. Box 948, Fremantle
Western Australia 6959
www.vividpublishing.com.au

A catalogue record for this
book is available from the
National Library of Australia

Acknowledgments

I would like to acknowledge the work of Fontaine Publishing Group in editing and publishing this book. You are an amazing team.

I would like to acknowledge the hard work of my late mother, Margaret, who invented her own form of physiotherapy that enabled me to walk again after contracting polio. Mama, I will always remember you as the strong, smart, kind and loving woman that you were. It's because of you that I am the strong woman I am today.

I would like to thank the Australian government for granting me a refugee visa, which enabled me to enter and live in Australia, for granting me citizenship to become an Australian, for allowing me access to Medicare and welfare, and for providing me with rent-subsidised housing. Australia has become my home and I am proud to call myself an Australian.

Thank you, Australia, for welcoming me with open arms.

I would like to thank the Aboriginal people for allowing me to enter their country, Australia, and for allowing me to live in their land.

I would like to thank the Australian Refugee Association of South Australia for helping me resettle in Australia.

I would like to thank the University of South Australia for making Magill Campus accessible to me by providing me with a wheelchair to use in and around the university campus.

I would like to thank Disability SA, the Independent Living Centre, for providing me with an electric wheelchair to use in my home and community.

I would like to thank my sister, Angelina, and her husband, Dickson, for proposing that I come to Australia.

I would like to thank Dignity Party South Australia for allowing me to run with them for Parliament in the Upper House, in 2014 and 2018, to represent people with disabilities in South Australia.

I would like to thank Father Mario for blessing me with education.

I would like to thank my psychologist for helping me overcome the trauma I experienced in my childhood, in the refugee camps, and for helping me deal with the effects of rape.

I would like to thank the South Sudanese Kuku community, the Equatorian community, the Dinka community and all the other African communities in South Australia, for welcoming me into your communities and for making me feel at home.

I would like to thank all my friends in Australia —Kristy, Karen, Anna, Stan, and David A — for your support over the years and for standing by my side.

I would like to thank Life Christian Centre in Adelaide for your prayers and support.

I would like to thank Alex, the father of my kids, for your support.

And finally, to you, my beautiful daughters, Destiny, eight years old, and Dorcas, two and a half years old, this book is dedicated to you. I love you so much.

One

Introduction

I was an ordinary little four-year-old girl called Esther with an extraordinary life journey ahead of me. I was the youngest of six children, with three sisters and two brothers. My father and brother were both killed during the Sudan civil war. One of my sisters also died after contracting liver disease in Oliji refugee camp in Uganda in 1992. My brother lives in South Sudan, one sister lives in Australia, and another sister lives in Uganda.

I was born in Kajo-Keji, South Sudan, in the early eighties; I was a normal bubbly baby girl, full of life. It was a home birth in a village where there was no medical attention and no midwives. Some villages in Africa have medically trained professionals to help with home births. But these midwives do not have medical equipment on standby to help them. They are helpless if anything does go wrong during or after childbirth. Some villages, like mine, are very far from any hospital or medical centre, and it might take two to four days' walk to get to a hospital. The sick person might die before seeing a doctor. There were no ambulance services where I was born, and even if there had been cars, they would have been of no use, as there were no roads.

If any of us were sick, my mother, Margaret, would treat us with local herbs. For those who could afford treatment, a visit to a witch doctor would be their only hope of cure. The witch doctors would ask for a lot of money; for those with no money, they would demand livestock, like goats or chickens, to pay for the treatment. Although they might be able to treat some illnesses, some of them were fake doctors who were only interested in taking people's money and livestock. They might allege that a family member had bewitched the sick person, and that was why they were sick. Suspicion and loss of trust would then tear the family apart.

One fateful morning in Kajo-Keji, I woke up with a high fever and a body paralysed from neck to toe. I was not able to stand or sit up. My mother gave me a medicine made from local herbs, and invented a physiotherapy treatment. She tied my hands to two poles to support me, and left me to stand there for an hour every morning and evening for two or three months. I had to learn to sit and to walk again, and I eventually regained strength in my upper body. Thanks to my mother, who worked tirelessly, I was able to walk again, though with great difficulty.

I was about four years old when I was struck by poliomyelitis. There was no immunisation available to families in South Sudan. I was left with a weak lower back, a deformed and painful right foot, and a very weak left leg. I now suffer from post-polio syndrome, which is associated with headaches, muscle and bone ache, fatigue, and general body exhaustion. I limp, and have a lot of falls. I use a wheelchair outside of the house to access the community.

I am from the South Sudanese Kuku/Bari speaking group, and I speak the Kuku language and English. My parents were divorced when I was just four years old; after this, I lived with my mother and her relatives in the village of Lomura before we fled to Uganda as refugees, and then finally to Australia.

I am a survivor of rape. In July 2002, I was raped by a friend in Uganda. I was twenty years old at the time of the rape. I will call the man who raped me Ben. I was in my sister's house, helping in her retail shop when I first came to know Ben. The rape happened when I was in my cousin's house in Kampala, Uganda.

My cousin lived four streets away from Ben. Before the rape, my sister and I had an argument and she pushed me. I fell on the ground on my knee and I hurt my right knee. I was upset and in pain, so I went to my cousin's house for two weeks to cool off. I had also planned to visit my cousin to tell him that I would be travelling to Kyangwali refugee camp in a few weeks' time. This would be the first time I would go to a refugee camp by myself.

At the time, I felt like everyone around me except Ben disliked me. I felt like Ben was the only person who understood me. The first time I met Ben was at the shop. His cousin Jack, who was a good customer in my sister's shop and a friend of my sister's family, introduced Ben to me at the shop. I came to know Ben better in the Church choir at Kampala. Ben visited my sister's house a few times with Jack, and later alone. Ben became a good friend of mine and of my sister's family.

Ben told me that he was drawn to me because I reminded him of his younger brother John in South Sudan, who also had a physical disability. He said that he would introduce me to John soon, when he came to visit. Ben was very proud of John, as he was a strong outspoken young man with a disability, and like me, he didn't allow his disability to define him. Ben said that he was proud of me too. That was the first time someone had said that to me. On many occasions, Ben compared me to his brother, and he said that he was going to organise for the two of us (me and John) to get together and talk about how we could help other South Sudanese people with disabilities who have a voice, but want encouragement to use their voice.

Ben was attracted to my voice, and he said to me a few times jokingly that he was going to marry me so that I could sing him to sleep every night. Ben made me feel comfortable around him, and I trusted him. I guess I was starting to develop feelings for him, but we were not in a relationship. I started thinking what life would be like for me if I lived with him. My cousin, niece and I visited Ben a few times in his house when John was there, and he cooked meals for us. He was a good cook.

John and I got along really well, and we became friends. John was interested in music like me, and we sang together every time we were in Ben's house. One afternoon in July 2002, Ben invited me to his house to say goodbye to John, who was returning to Yei in South Sudan the following day. I went to Ben's house, hoping to sing one last song with John before he returned to South Sudan. I went alone this time, as the invitation was at short notice. When I got there, I found that Ben was the only person in the house, and as always, he was cooking. Ben welcomed me and made a cup of tea for me. Ben told me that John, Jack and his other brother Peter from Kenya had gone to his aunt's house to say goodbye to her. He reassured me that John would be back home soon. He played a very beautiful Gospel song, first on the guitar and then on a CD, to keep me entertained while I waited for John. I felt at home and I sang along. I didn't suspect anything at all.

Suddenly, Ben turned off his charcoal stove and he increased the volume. Some of his neighbours were playing loud music at the time too. Ben grabbed me from the back and dragged me to his bed. He forced me onto the bed and ripped my nickers off me.

I tried to fight him, but he overpowered me and pinned me onto the bed with his arms and elbows. I screamed, but nobody came to my aid. Ben covered my mouth with his hand, and he yelled at me, telling me to be quiet. He said that if I tried to fight him and screamed again, he would hurt me. He pulled his trousers down and he forced himself onto me. He penetrated me by force, causing physical injuries while I was screaming and saying, "You are hurting me!" Several minutes later, he got up and pulled up his trousers. I sat on the bed sobbing, bleeding and terrified. I was a virgin no longer.

He sat back on the bed and asked, "Do you remember

that time I told you that I was going to marry you so you can sing for me?" I said nothing. He said that he meant it—he was going to marry me. He told me to stay on his bed and not move or make a noise. He said that if I co-operated, he would not hurt me, but if I caused trouble, I would be hurt. He left the house and went across the road to a boutique. I tried to escape and ask for help, but the door was locked. He had locked me inside his house. I was terrified. I thought that he was going to kill me, so I sat back on the bed, still sobbing. He came back with new African clothes for himself. He told me that if I behaved, he would buy good clothes for me like the ones he had just bought, and that he would take good care of me. He went to have a shower and wore his new clothes in front of me as a sign of celebration for raping a virgin.

I was still sitting on the bed, wondering what to do next. When he had finished dressing, he asked me to leave. He said that he was going to his aunt's house to see why his brothers hadn't come back. John was to catch the bus back to South Sudan later that night. It was 4 p.m. He convinced me that he would see me later at my cousin's house to discuss the next step. He opened the door to let me out, and there were his brothers at the door. He told his brothers that he was going to walk me down the road, and he would be back soon. It was plain that he had to get me out of there quickly because he feared what Jack would say, what he would make of the whole situation. So he walked me a few metres away from his house, then his face changed into that of a monster. He was angry. He threatened to kill me and my family if I ever told anyone about what happed. He told me that he was a member of the Sudan People's Liberation Army, the SPLA, and that he had a gun in his house. He said that he was going to use his gun to kill me and my relatives.

I went to my cousin's house and told my niece that Ben had raped me, and she told me not to tell my cousin so he wouldn't throw me out. She said that she would find a way of telling him. My niece was around the same age as me. My cousin was not in the house at the time. When he returned in the evening, my niece told him what had happened to me, and he asked me to leave.

I was bleeding and in pain. I could hardly walk. My face, throat, and body ached. My face, right eye, and top lip were sore and swollen the following day. I don't remember if Ben hit me on the face, or if it was from pinning me down on the bed. I felt dirty, and I needed to take several showers a day to make me feel clean. I felt violated, betrayed, ashamed and humiliated. I felt worthless, disempowered and less of a human. I felt guilty for going there alone.

Ben was in his late thirties. I later learnt that he was married with a child back in South Sudan.

My cousin took me back to my sister's house. My sister said that rape did not take place, that I had prostituted myself, and because of that, I was no longer welcome in her house. She found out from talking to other people that Ben was married to a woman who died of HIV/AIDS in the hospital in Uganda. She packed my things and took me to the bus. She took me back to my mother in Ibakwe refugee camp to die, because she thought I was HIV positive. My niece went back to Ben's house the following day to confront him, but Ben denied ever raping me. He said that maybe someone raped me on my way back to my cousin's after I left his house. He threatened to kill my niece if she didn't stop ruining his reputation.

My niece returned the following day and found Ben's house empty. She asked the neighbours, who reported that Ben had left for South Sudan early that morning. I never saw Ben again until recently on Facebook. I sent him a message asking if he remembered me, but he didn't respond. I wanted him to respond and tell me why he raped me, and what had happened to our two-year friendship. I wanted closure. I did try to find him a few times in Uganda and after arriving in Australia, but my search for him wasn't successful. I was informed in Australia in 2006 that he was working at the airport in Khartoum, North Sudan. I rang Khartoum airport a few times, and I finally got through to someone who claimed to have known him; she reported that Ben was in Juba, South Sudan. She said that when she saw him again, she would ask him to ring me. I left my number, but he never rang me back. I just wanted to ask him—why?

I returned to Kampala three weeks later and sought refuge in the Church. The pastor and my friend who lived near the Church asked me to leave the following day. They said that the man did nothing wrong and that I caused the rape, if it really did happen. They said that I was giving the Church a bad image. I went back to my sister's house and then to Kyangwali refugee camp four weeks later. My sister allowed me back to her house after some relatives in Moyo District, Northern Uganda, and in Ibakwe refugee camp, condemned her and her husband for the way they treated me after the rape. My sister's husband said that the rape didn't take place, that it was a plan gone wrong. Other people in the community, who heard about my rape, even those who didn't know me, said that my disability and the calamity that is written all over my face caused the rape. They said that bad things keep happening to me because disability brings calamity, and that wherever I go, calamity will always follow me.

My family, my Church and my friends in Uganda all said that the man did nothing wrong. Other people said that it was not rape, that I had prostituted myself! Even as I write now, there is still rape going on in Uganda and in South Sudan. Ben went unpunished for what he did, because nobody believed me.

Before long, rumours started circulating in my community that I was HIV positive because I had "slept" with a man who was infected with the virus. My friends, my Church, and some family members disowned me because they did not want to be associated with a prostitute, with someone who was HIV positive. I had a test done and was relieved to find out that I was HIV negative.

There were no people I knew in my community who had HIV/AIDS. There were, however, many Ugandans I knew who were reported to have the virus or who confessed to it, and were raising awareness and educating people in the community to keep themselves safe by abstaining from unsafe sex. My understanding at the time was that HIV/AIDS was spread by rich men having unprotected intercourse with vulnerable and poor women, who would then infect others. I guess because Ben was rich, and I was poor, people automatically concluded that he was HIV positive. HIV/AIDS prevention was part of the curriculum in primary and secondary schools in Uganda. People who were HIV/AIDS positive were going to schools and events to share their experiences with the public. The public was encouraged to use condoms to prevent the spread of HIV/AIDS.

Because nobody believed me, I was terrified to report the rape to the police in Uganda. Besides, the man who raped me was a rich man who could bribe the police. In Uganda, money talks. Reporting the rape to the police would have humiliated me still further and left me more heartbroken.

Now, I am proud that I reported the rape to my family, my Church and my friends, even though people didn't believe me. If I hadn't reported it, I would not be able to talk about it now, and I might have taken this secret with me to my grave. I want to encourage other young girls and women who are survivors of rape, especially women with disabilities, to speak out, regardless of whether people will believe them or not.

For a long time after the rape, I felt unclean, and I felt that I needed to take showers several times a day to make me clean. But the showers only made me physically clean; I still felt emotionally and psychologically broken and dirty. It was only after I came to Australia in 2005 (three years after the rape) that I was able to seek professional support. But it was not until 2008 that I started seeing a psychologist, which has helped me to deal with the effects of the rape.

Now, I feel empowered that I can use my rape experience to help other women out there who are in my position. I also now know that it was not my fault that Ben raped me.

Growing up in the South Sudanese culture as a child with a disability was traumatising. People with disabilities, in South Sudan and Africa generally, not only have the physical and mental effects of being less able than others, but also are treated as second class humans and disadvantaged in many ways in their communities. They are not involved in any decision-making processes; choices and decisions are made for them. Girls with disabilities in the South Sudanese culture are kept invisible in the family home. They are considered an embarrassment to the family.

There is so much ignorance about disability in Africa and in the South Sudanese community in particular. People with disabilities are believed to bring calamity to their families and communities, and may suffer barbaric treatment by those who are more able. Some African communities disown women who have children with disabilities. In other parts of Africa, women with disabilities and those with children with disabilities are not allowed to use public transport. Those with no disability refuse to sit near people with disabilities in the bus because they are considered dirty. People with big egos do not want to be associated with people with a disability, as they believe this will make them less human.

Parents of girls living with disabilities in Africa may choose men in the community to rape their daughters over and over again until they become pregnant, so that they have children of their own, who are expected to take care of their disabled mothers. This act is not considered to be sexual abuse in African culture. On the contrary, it is considered to be an act of kindness to the woman. In the South Sudanese culture, disability is seen as a curse, possession by a bad spirit, and the result of witchcraft.

I am grateful that my mother did not abandon or disown me because of my disability. Yet many parents of children with disabilities in Africa find it difficult to accept disability, and relinquish their caring role.

Talking about private, personal and family issues to professionals like psychologists, counsellors, legal professionals, and even to family members, is considered taboo in the South Sudanese culture. Children like me who are victims of domestic violence and abuse are left with no support, and suffer long-term mental health issues. Name-calling about my disability was the order of the day, making me feel ashamed and disempowered. I was called *bata* (lame person); *Padangu mokosi* described my deformed legs and feet; I was called "evil spirit," and "calamity."

There were also names related to me having no father and male figure at home. Having no father was a taboo in my village unless your dad was dead. Usually what people do in my village is to arrange for the brother or an older male relative to marry a woman whose husband is dead, to keep the children of the deceased in the family home. Having no father was considered abnormal. For most of my childhood, I felt as though I lived in a nutshell. I was constantly told and reminded that a low life was my fate. For many years I accepted and embraced that lifestyle, being put down, feeling worthless, ugly, unwanted. I thought that living a low life in a nutshell was my future. But one day, when I was twenty years old, I woke up. I realised that living in a nutshell was *not* my lifestyle, it was just what people thought of me, and I finally cracked out of my shell.

After I completed secondary school studies in Uganda, I took courage and started challenging my own thoughts and those of others about having and living with a disability; that is how I broke out of my shell. I have since become a social worker specialising in human rights, giving voice to the voiceless and to those with a voice who need encouragement to use their voice. I am an advocate for those who cannot speak for themselves, especially people with disabilities and South Sudanese women. I want to see that people with disabilities are treated with respect, are included in society, and have equal access to opportunities, jobs, education, resources, and services in the community. I also believe that women with disabilities can have healthy children of their own who do not have disabilities. Therefore, the rights and dignity of women with disabilities should not be taken away from them by medical professionals, who may make decisions to sterilise women with disabilities without their consent, in the belief that they will have children with disabilities or that they may not be able to look after them properly. Although sterilisation might be the only option for some women with disabilities, this method should not be imposed on every woman with a disability.

I am a woman with a physical disability, yet I have two beautiful, healthy daughters. Still, some people ask me if my daughters also have polio. Some think that polio can be inherited from the parent, which is not true. Polio is not genetic and it is not contagious. When I was young, before I became pregnant with my first child, people had a lot of theories about me. Some said that I would not be able to have children because of my disability, and others told me that I would not be able to carry a pregnancy to full term because of my scoliosis, my weak back and weak legs. Others told me that even if I were able to have children, I would not be able to look after them because of my disability!

I looked at them, and I said, watch me! People told me to work hard and save enough money to adopt a child, but I told them that I would have children of my own, and now, I am a proud mother of two beautiful daughters. Against all odds, I went on to have three pregnancies; unfortunately, I lost my second daughter to stillbirth. She was born premature in June 2015 and she died few minutes after she was born. I want to clarify: the premature birth of my daughter had nothing to do with the fact that I have a disability. God had his own reasons for taking her away from me so early in her life.

When I was pregnant with my first daughter, I had people lined up waiting to take my baby away from me, because they thought that I would not be able to look after her, but I proved that I am capable of looking after my children regardless of my disability.

I am happy to say that I am still able to raise my two beautiful girls alone without any help from anybody. I remember lying down on the hospital bed two weeks after my first child was born, wondering if I would ever be allowed to take her home with me, as the doctors were not in any hurry to discharge me. Two weeks later, I was discharged, but the occupational therapist from the Women's and Children's Hospital in Adelaide followed me home. He came fifteen minutes after I had arrived home to determine whether my house was a suitable environment for my baby to live in. They had assumed that because I was a young single mother with a disability and from a refugee background, I couldn't afford a clean and decent house to raise my daughter in. The occupational therapist was blown away when he saw that I had my house set up ready for my baby. I had a bassinet, a bed and other baby gear all in place before I went to the hospital to have her. I gathered that the occupational therapist was prepared to make arrangements to take my baby away from me there and then, but because I was able to prove to him that disability is not inability, I got to keep my baby. If you put your mind to something, your determination will help you to achieve your goals in life, regardless of your disability, mental illness, medical condition or any other limitation.

I believe that disability is not *inability*; therefore people with disabilities should be given the chance to explore new opportunities that will enable them to reach their full potential. With a positive mindset, people with disabilities can function independently or with assistance, when they are given the right kind of support.

Two

Life in 'Beliyak, South Sudan

My parents were peasants from Kajo-Keji in South
Sudan, and we lived on the food they could grow.
They had a small piece of land where they grew okra,
Molokia, groundnuts (peanuts), cassava, sweet potatoes,
pumpkin, beans, and peas, especially black eye peas,
and any other vegetables they could find. Meat and
sugar were luxuries in my family. I didn't have any toys
to play with when I was a child.

My father also worked as a primary school teacher
at a local school, and later he worked as a cleaner in a
hospital, but he wasn't getting paid enough money to
care for his family and to pay his children's school fees.
You would think that my dad would use the little money
from his salary on food, clothing, and education for his
children, but instead he used his money for alcohol.
There were no services in our village to help alcoholics

to quit and to stay sober. My siblings had to work for other richer people in the village by harvesting their garden produce to pay for their school fees. The aim was to work for the rich people in return for money, but they were not paid cash after a long day's hard work. Instead, they were given a small portion of whatever they had harvested from the rich man's garden to go and sell in their local market, to get money for their school fees. Going to the market to sell the produce is hard work on top of a day's hard work. Child labour in my village was not defined as child abuse. Survival of the fittest was the order of the day; therefore, everybody had to work, not just to chip in, but to earn a living.

You are probably asking yourself, how in the world did I manage to pay my own school fees, given my physical disability? Well, keep reading, and I will tell you about my schooling later in this book.

My mother didn't have the opportunity to pursue an education because the South Sudanese cultural practice was that women and girls were only trained to be mothers, housewives, and family or community carers. But she was a very clever woman, a strong woman, and she was generous, loving, kind, and caring.

My father made some choices in his life that I'm sure he wasn't proud of. He drank too much alcohol and he abused his family physically, financially and emotionally. Repeatedly, my mother had her head pinned to the wall and bashed against it; she was hit with objects, including furniture, and anything that my father could use as a weapon, and hot food was poured on her head. She often had her throat squeezed, leaving her with severe bruising, a black eye, and a swollen face. Sometimes she would stop breathing because of the beating and the strangling, but she survived the ongoing trauma.

My siblings and I did not escape the violence. There were times when the bush became a home and a refuge for me and my mother and my siblings. As the violence escalated, my two brothers decided that they no longer wanted to be part of the abuse and trauma, so they ran away from home when I was a baby, leaving their four little sisters and their mother to survive as best we could.

Physical, emotional, and financial abuse, and any other type of abuse perpetrated by men against their wives, women and children, was not defined or called "domestic violence or abuse" in our village. It was called punishment for women's and children's bad behaviour.

Like thousands of other unfortunate children in the world, I was a victim of domestic violence, which left permanent emotional scars in my life. Whereas, in the Western world, there may be social services to care for abused children who are victims of domestic violence, there was no welfare agency in my village to care for me and my siblings while the abuse was happening. My siblings and my mother and I were physically, financially, and emotionally abused, as well as socially isolated and neglected by my father. I was not allowed to interact or play with other children in my father's village. My family became a hot topic of gossip in the village because of the ongoing domestic violence and our poor living conditions. As time went by and the physical abuse became uncontrollable, like other children who are victims of domestic violence, my sisters and I lost respect for our father and fought him, throwing rocks and other objects at him, as well as hitting him with pieces of wood and metal while he was beating our mother. We screamed and made a lot of noise, repeatedly calling out for help. But we were too young to protect her.

"Help us, he is killing her!" we would scream, while he was pushing our mother's head against the wall and choking her. But nobody came to our rescue. Some neighbours had tried to intervene a few times in the past, but that made things worse, so they stopped coming to help. We thought that the screaming and the loud noises would make our father stop hurting our mother, but it didn't work.

My mother stayed in this abusive relationship for many years because she feared losing her children. In the South Sudanese culture, children belong to men, and women are considered to be a man's property. Eventually, my mother decided to leave without us, with the hope that we would one day look for her and find her alive and well.

Our local community, neighbours, relatives, and friends in South Sudan were not able to stop the abuse or resolve the dispute, as it only happened when my father was drunk, and it was impossible to get sense out of him when he was like that. Drug and alcohol or mental health services would have been the answer, but the village did not have these services.

One morning in 'Beliyak after the local market day, I woke up and my mother was gone. I thought that she had slept in the market place, so I went and asked my dad.

"Baba, Where is Mama?"

"Your mother is gone and you will never see her again," he said.

"No she is not! She went to the market and she will be back."

"Your mother is not coming back, Esther; she is gone for good."

"Why? Who is going to give me food?"

"Your mother is a bad woman and she does not

deserve you."

"I want Mama!" I cried, jumping up and down.

"Do not even think of going to stay with your mother. Because if you do, you WILL SUFFER, and you will starve to death. Your mother is not able to look after you without me. She needs me to be able to care for you," he said.

After hearing him talk, I left the room and ran outside. I sat on the dirt at the back of the house, singing the songs that my mother used to sing to me, and I cried quietly for a long time.

But the songs did not bring my mother back.

I thought that my mother was still at the market and that she would come home, but she didn't come back. I had to face the reality of growing up without my mother.

I was sad, angry and guilty. If I hadn't been naughty, my mother would not have left me. If my older siblings had fought harder and had defeated my dad, my mother would not have left us.

I didn't know that it was not my fault that my mother had left. I didn't see that my siblings were only kids and that there was nothing they could have done to stop the violence. I wanted to bring my mother back, but I was too young to do so. Besides, I didn't know where she had gone.

After Mama left, my sister, Selina, who was eight years old, ran away from home too. She was lucky enough to find her way to the market, and someone who knew our mum took her to our mother's village, where they were reunited. Angelina and Edith, who were also kids at the time, about ten and twelve years old, took over our mother's caring role when our dad was out. He was never home most of the time. Angelina and Edith walked for miles to fetch water and firewood, and they cooked meals. But things were no longer the same in our family home, because our mother was irreplaceable. My mother knew what to do in emergency situations and she knew how to put food on the table. Although Angelina and Edith were able to cook and care for me and for themselves, they were not able to provide a meal every day of the week like our mother did. So we survived on one meal a day if we were lucky. Mostly, we only ate three to four days a week, and we didn't eat the other days at all.

One wet and cold night after my mother had left, my father beat up Angelina and Edith after returning home drunk and finding no food in the house. After beating my sisters, he went inside to grab a weapon, but we ran away and hid in a nearby bush. We waited for some time to make sure that our father wasn't following us or roaming around looking for us. We feared returning home to our father more than spending the night outdoors, so we spent a wet and cold night in the bush with no raincoats, no warm clothes, and no blankets to cover ourselves. We were washed by heavy rains and bitten by mosquitoes. To top it all, there were wild animals, including lions, hyenas, wild pigs, and wild cats roaming around the bush, and they roared all night. We were terrified, but we had nothing else we could do and no one else to turn to. So we prayed to God for a miracle and for a safe return home when our father had sobered up a bit. Even then, returning home the following morning was more terrifying than sleeping in the bush.

This was our first time of sleeping in the bush without our mother. Mum always knew what to do in situations like this, but on this occasion, we had to work things out for ourselves.

"It's raining heavily, what are we going to do?" whispered Edith.

"We are going to sleep here," whispered Angelina.

"I want to go home," I shouted, shivering terribly.

"Shhhhhhhhhhh, keep quiet," whispered Edith.

"Don't you shh…. me, I am wet and cold, and I want to go home," I said.

"It's alright, Esther you will be fine here," whispered Edith.

I was scared of my father, but even more scared of sleeping in the bush without my mother. But my two sisters managed to calm me down. Angelina was severely bruised, with swollen face and eyes. She was injured and bleeding from the beating, and decided that we should not sleep together. She reasoned that she should isolate herself from her two little sisters because of her injuries, as she thought that the wild animals might smell the blood on her body, and they might go in the direction of the smell, and she might become their late night dinner. Angelina told Edith to spend the night with me and to be quiet even if an animal approached, scared or attacked us.

Angelina left and hid a few metres away from us. Edith, (who died in Uganda refugee camp during the Sudan civil war), took care of me throughout the wet and cold night. Each time we heard an animal roaring or approaching, Edith would push me onto the ground, lie on top of me, and would cover my mouth with her hands to stop me from screaming. Edith did this all night to protect me, so that if we were to be attacked or eaten by wild animals, she would be killed and eaten first, and hopefully, I would survive to tell the story— like I am doing now. Despite all that happened that night, God protected us, and we returned home safely the following morning, though we had headaches and malaria.

One morning, I woke up with a very weak body, and was wobbly and drowsy after spending the day and the night before without a meal, as Angelina and Edith were too tired to cook and there was nothing to cook anyway.

"Esther, wake up," said Angelina. "No, I don't want to," I said.

"Why?" Angelina asked.

"I feel weak."

"Wake up, brush your teeth and wash your face so you can have some porridge," said Angelina.

"Ok," I said happily. I got up, but I stumbled and fell back onto the floor on my bottom.

"Ouch, my bottom." I was shaking, and I shouted, "I need some water to drink."

"Go to the pot and get some drinking water by yourself," said Angelina.

"No I can't; I am weak."

"Yes you can; the longer you waste time lying down there the weaker you will get," said Edith, who was doing the dishes.

"No I can't; I'm weak and I'll fall into the pot. Get me some water please!"

At first my sisters thought that I was joking. They laughed at me, but when they saw that I was really weak, shaking, sweating and unable to stand up, Edith rushed to get some water and she gave me some to drink. I was dehydrated and going into shock. But Angelina fed me some porridge, and I drank more water after eating the porridge. I recovered quickly, and I went outside to play an hour after eating the porridge.

In our isolation, my sisters and I were not allowed to attend any of the South Sudanese Kuku cultural functions or community events in my father's village, including child naming and marriage ceremonies, and traditional Kuku seasonal dances. Before our parents' divorce, I used to go to Church sometimes with my mother, and I enjoyed Sunday School Services and I was in the Sunday School Choir. But after Mama left, I stopped attending Church. My sisters stopped going to school. Instead, we gardened and grew crops for our food, like Mama used to do. My job was to watch the garden and make noises all day to scare the monkeys away from eating the crops. With this severe isolation, I became withdrawn. I had lost hope that my life would change.

The next time I saw my mother was several months later, when she came home with some people, and possessions were divided between my parents. I didn't know why there were so many people in my home and why possessions were divided and why my parents didn't fight on this particular day. I was used to living in a violent environment, and I thought that physical fights, quarrelling, shouting, yelling, screaming, and smashing things was the normal way of living and growing up. So I was expecting a fight when my mother came back that day. I was told that my mother was never coming back again, and that I could not live with her, and I didn't know why. So Mama left without me again.

Before my mother returned to take things, my dad had instructed me not to go anywhere near my mum and not to say anything to her, otherwise I would be in big trouble, so I didn't speak to my mum that afternoon. I didn't understand why I wasn't allowed to talk to my mum or why I wasn't allowed to go with her, but now I understand. In the Kuku culture, children belong to their dad, and women are considered to be men's property. My mother couldn't take me and my sisters with her because of this cultural belief and practices. I was angry that my mother left twice without me, and this impacted on my relationship with my mother. I thought that she didn't love me. My experience with my mum has made me be a better mum myself. There were times when I could have left my children, but I would never leave them. I have stayed with my kids through the tough times and I love them to bits.

A few months after their possessions were divided between my parents, my sisters and I were finally reunited with my mother in her village. During this time, my father had become too ill to care for us. After a night of heavy drinking, he had woken up the following morning in the bush with his mouth full of black ants. The ants had chewed his throat and stomach so badly that he needed months or years of recovery, as he had to learn how to speak and eat again.

Three
Life in Lomura Village, South Sudan

My mother's village, Lomura in Kajo-Keji, South Sudan, was beautiful, with lots of mango trees and fruits and beautiful vegetation. It was green with lots of rain throughout the year, and it had very fertile soil. My mother and my siblings, being girls, could only cultivate a small piece of land, and they planted a few seeds here and there, but they had a big harvest each year. Although I didn't have a father or brothers to provide food, shelter, and security, I never went hungry in Lomura Village, because we always had enough food to feed us throughout the year.

Winter was the best time of the year in Lomura village, as I got to meet new people on social occasions such as traditional marriage ceremonies, child naming ceremonies and other South Sudanese–Kuku traditional functions that took place in winter. Winter afternoons in Lomura Village were hot and dry. The winter season starts in December and goes until the end of March. Winter was also the only time when I had the chance to hear the South Sudanese-Kuku traditional stories, old generational stories as well as new ones, around the open wood fire. During winter, my family and our close neighbours and elders sat together around the fire early in the mornings and late in the evenings or during the night, and we were told traditional educational stories. Winter mornings and evenings were very cold and dry in Lomura village, so we had open wood fires in the homes and we all sat around the fire to warm ourselves up. Sitting around the wood fire during the winter season in Kajo-Keji was one of the most important cultural activities.

There were only two seasons in Lomura village, winter and summer. Summer starts in April and finishes in November, and this is the time when there is lots of heavy rain. Summer is also the time for gardening, planting, and harvesting. The winter season in Lomura is also a time when women and children take part in arts and crafts. Women and girls get together and sit under mango trees to knit tablecloths and bed sheets, weave and make baskets and mats, as well as dress each other's hair. The women gossip and share their personal stories with each other during these activities.

My young age didn't stop me from participating in the arts and crafts activities. I learned basket weaving, mat making, and hair dressing skills from the women and girls in Lomura village. My interest, confidence and determination meant that the skills I learned there stayed with me, and I became a hairdresser later, in the refugee camps in Uganda. I now dress my daughters' hair, to save money where possible.

Because there was no milling machine in Lomura village to grind maize, millet, sorghum, and cassava into semolina or flour, women and girls in Lomura village ground grains into flour, using big grinding stones with their bare hands. There was a small stone that the women held tightly, grinding the maize on a big grinding stone. During winter, women and girls got to grind flour in groups; this activity is known in the South Sudanese-Kuku language as *jijo `yi lele*, which means grinding in a group on big stones. Women in Lomura village use the maize, cassava, millet and sorghum flour for making porridge in the morning for breakfast and also for making *`diloŋ* (semolina) for lunch and dinner. Semolina is like mashed potato that you can eat with stews.

Grinding flour is a very important educational activity that is used to train girls and teenagers, to prepare them for the caring role, so that when they are married, they will be able to provide food for their children, husbands, and the extended family at large. I used to follow my sisters to the flour grinding activity, and grind small semolina on a small grinding stone using my bare hands. I enjoyed spending time with my sisters and their friends and our neighbours' children during the flour grinding activity. When girls and young women come together in Lomura village to the flour grinding activity and to do arts and crafts, they often talk about relationship issues, and they compose meaningful traditional songs in Kuku language, telling stories about the boys and men they are in love with, or stories about their failed and broken relationships.

The South Sudanese–Kuku teenage girls in Lomura village slept in groups of four to six in a one-room grass-thatched house. Sleeping in groups is called *toto `yi doro* in the South Sudanese–Kuku language; it is almost like sleepovers in Australia. The only difference is that the teenagers in Lomura village could choose a place where they would sleep for weeks, months or even years, not just for the weekend or overnight. Like the flour grinding activity, girls who slept in groups would tell stories about their boyfriends and compose relationship songs. Sleeping in groups was not only a way of getting teenagers to socialise and talk about teenage issues among themselves, but it also gave them the chance to go to the night club, where they could meet boys. Like any other parents, some parents in my village refused to let their girls get involved in any nightclubs, including discos and traditional dance clubs. The only way girls from such families would socialise with boys was to sleep in a group, and sometimes sneak out to a dancing club at night, mostly at the weekend. But if they were caught, they would be punished severely for disobeying their parents. These girls walked for miles to go dancing, and they loved doing it. I was too young to go to nightclubs, so I slept in my mother's room.

As part of the South Sudanese–Kuku culture, girls and boys, mostly teenagers, were encouraged to build small grass-thatched houses at the back of their parents' houses, and they lived in these houses during the day for the whole of the winter season. These small teenage houses were called *kelekende*, and some called them *slams*. Up to twenty kids (boys and girls) would live in the slams for the whole winter season. The older girls and boys in the group played the role of mothers and fathers to the younger boys and girls, providing food and taking care of them. This was a very important traditional educational practice that gave the boys and girls the opportunity to learn to be a husband, a wife, a mum, or a dad. It was a good way for girls to learn how to cook and for boys to learn how to build houses, and how to hunt for meat and to provide for their families.

Winter in Lomura was the season for hunting. A group of men and women would go to the bush and stay there for days or weeks to hunt for wild animals, and they would return home with wild animal meat. The women's role was to cook for the men while they were in the bush. It is clear that South Sudanese men function better with women by their side. It is true of this culture, too, that "behind every successful man, there is a woman." Traditionally, cooking was not a man's role in the South Sudanese–Kuku culture. This was why men had to take their women with them when they went hunting. However, this cultural pattern has changed, especially here in Australia, where some South Sudanese–Kuku men are now involved in house chores and childcare activities, while their wives go to work, study, or attend appointments. Gender roles are gradually changing for South Sudanese men and women in the Western world.

Being displaced from Lomura village because of the Sudan civil war meant that I lost all the traditional activities, as well as my community, relatives, friends, and the beautiful land that I had fallen in love with. War tears cultures apart and makes countries poor. I do not know if Lomura will ever be the same again; some of the people from my village have integrated into other cultures in Uganda, Kenya, and other countries in the Western world, so our culture has now been diluted. Even if some of the South Sudanese–Kuku people who lived in Lomura village before the war were to return there, things will never be the same again. Most of the older Kuku people who used to tell traditional stories in Lomura died during the war, and most of the young former residents have now integrated into other cultures and have now forgotten their stories, which were not written down.

Four

My First Day of School

My three sisters went to Logu Primary School in South Sudan, but my mother would not let me go to school because of my mobility impairment. Logu village was some distance from our village, which did not have a primary school. Mama was also worried that I would be bullied at school because of my disability. Several times, I asked my mother if I could go to school, and she said no. One afternoon, when I was six years old, I went to my aunt's house and asked my cousin Modong, who was about the same age as me, if she would take me to school with her the next day. She said yes! I went home with a happy smiley face after we had planned my escape to school the next morning. Modong told me to be ready early in the morning. I could not wait to go to school, and I wished the night would not come, so I could go to school right away.

Early next morning, when it was still dark, Modong came to my house and hid by the tree at the side of the house. She waited for my mother to go out into the garden and for my sisters to go to school.

A few minutes later, after everyone was gone, Modong peeped in through the door and whispered, "Esther, are you ready?"

"Yes I'm ready," I said.

"Come, let us go before your mother comes back home," said Modong.

"Okay, let's go," I replied, and off we went. The walk took about two hours.

When we left home, the sun was not out. The sun came out while we were on our way. The road was full of sand during the dry season, and full of mud during the rainy season. The landscape was flat, with no hills. We passed through fields of maize, cassava, ground-nuts, crops, and other vegetation. There was short and long grass, and lots of big trees, including mango trees. We passed people's homes, where they were working in their gardens. People were walking and riding their bikes. Some of the areas on the road were quiet and scary because of the big long grasses and trees.

I took rests along the way when I needed it until we reached the school. I could walk for ten to fifteen minutes and then I would take a rest and walk again. But when I turned twenty-five years old, here in Australia, post-polio syndrome kicked in, and my mobility and muscle functioning started getting much worse. Now I can't walk for five minutes without resting and falling.

On my first day at school, I could not have been happier. I followed Modong to a class that was held under a tree. It was Year One, and we had English and Maths lessons. That day, I wrote in the dirt with my finger. Most people say that their journey begins with one foot in front of the other, but my journey started with a finger in the dirt.

Because we were late getting to school, I wasn't able to speak to the headmaster when we arrived. But I spoke to him during break after the first two lessons. The education system in South Sudan was not like the one in Australia. Here, most likely, you contact the school first, visit the school and talk to the business manager and the principal, attend a principal's or school tour, fill out enrolment forms, then wait for a letter to arrive in your letter box saying that your child has been accepted at the school, then you and your child will attend an interview with the teacher before your child can start. In my village, you just turned up and registered your child, and the child could start attending classes straight away, on the same day. In most cases, the child just rocked up like I did and enrolled themselves, without any adult accompanying them, and this was acceptable.

After the first two lessons, Modong introduced me to her class teacher, Ben. He took me to the headmaster's office to register. The headmaster was an older man, in his sixties. He was friendly, understanding and kind. He told me to go home and tell my father to come to school the next day to buy uniform and stationery for me, and to pay my school fees.

I hung my head and said, "I do not have a father". "Who is going to pay your school fees?" asked the headmaster.

"My older sister, Angelina, is a student in the high school here. I will ask her to come and talk to you," I explained.

The headmaster looked at me. He shook his head and took a deep breath. "I know your sisters. I will talk to Angelina. You can go back to class now." I was allowed to study for free, but I wasn't allowed to sit for the end of year exams until my school fees were paid.

When I came out of the headmaster's office, relieved and happy, I headed straight to the playground, where I played games. There were many games at school during break time, including netball, skipping, square games, soccer and twelve holes games. I sang and danced in a circle, and played the twelve holes game with the other children from my class.

I also managed to play the circle game, where we sang and moved around in circle. One person was outside of the circle and acted as a lion, and one person inside the circle acted as a lamb or a goat. The lion outside of the circle hunted the lamb or goat inside of the circle. The people forming the circle had to protect the little animal from the lion.

Modong was kind enough to share her lunch with me, as I didn't have any. I wrote my class work on the dirt with my finger under the tree, and I scored ten out of ten in maths. I thoroughly enjoyed my first day of school, and I knew that this was exactly where I belonged.

"Staying at home alone is boring," I said to Modong as we walked home. But I was a bit scared, going back home to my Mum after disobeying her.

We got home late after a long day at school. To my relief, Mum was happy to know that I was able to walk to school and back home safely. The following day and the days after, she was happy for me to keep going to school.

The school was for boys and girls, starting at 8 a.m. and finishing at 4 p.m. It took us about two hours to walk to school and two hours to walk home. There were no school buses, no community buses, and no public transport in Lomura village where we lived. People had to walk long distances to school, to the market, to the hospital, and to fetch water and firewood.

Sadly, after one-and-a-half years of studying in Logu primary school, my family was shattered and my school life interrupted by the Sudan Civil War, which had started in 1982.

Before fleeing to Uganda as a refugee thirty years ago, I lived in two villages in Kajo-Keji, South Sudan; 'Beliyak, my father's village, and then Lomura, my mother's village. There were many good and funny moments in my young life, as well as many hardships. In 'Beliyak village, before my parents separated, our family of six lived in a one-room grass-thatched house which could only fit one small hand-made bed. I and my three sisters slept on the floor on a big dry cow skin, with no blanket to cover us, and my parents slept on the bed, made of sorghum and bamboo sticks. We used the same room for cooking in the rainy season, using firewood, which produced a lot of smoke, for there was no chimney. It can be hard to breath in the small house with the smoke when it's raining. The smoke made my eyes stream with tears.

The second village we lived in in South Sudan, Lomura, had no borehole water. My mother and sisters collected water from a big, fast-flowing river, Ki'bo, which was about six kilometres away from home.

They carried the water on their heads in clay pots and jerrycans. In Lomura village, people also washed their clothes and bathed in the same river.

Five

The Sudan Civil War

As if my disability was not enough, the outbreak of the Sudan civil war in the early 1980s has had devastating effects on my life. To begin with, there was a lot of speculation in my village about men carrying guns, looting villages, raping women and young girls, and killing innocent people in South Sudan. What started as rumours became a war, which left many innocent South Sudanese people dead. I thought that people in my village were talking about something that was going to happen in many years to come. What I didn't know was that the war people were talking about was already happening.

I got the shock of my life when I started seeing unwanted visitors with guns raiding my village, robbing poor people of their food, money, peace and freedom. I was scared to death and I felt like hiding myself in a hole until the nightmare was over, but there was no hole to hide in, and this was no nightmare, but a real civil war.

I had to accept that the unwanted men with guns were destroying my beautiful village. These black men with guns were called the Sudan People's Liberation Army (the SPLA). I called them the Sudanese rebels. People in my village called them 'duŋö murut, which translates as neck slaughterers.

The first group of SPLA who entered our village were South Sudanese people known as the Equatorians; the Dinka and the other groups arrived later. The Dinka were the most feared group of SPLA in South Sudan. I didn't know why this was so. All I knew was that they were cruel, arrogant, merciless and brutal. Instead of the SPLA fighting the "enemy," (the Arabs) in the Northern part of Sudan, they took money, food, goats, chickens and more with them every time they came to our village. They robbed, looted, raped women and girls, and killed innocent people, leaving people with no food, terrified, and sometimes dead. Most of those killed were men. Many children were left without fathers, and others were left as orphans. Some of the SPLA abducted young boys from their homes and forced them to train as child soldiers. These children were then forced to go back to their villages to kill people, including their parents and relatives, and to burn down their own villages. A lot of the child soldiers were killed during the Sudan civil war, but others survived. For the survivors, their nightmare was not over. Many of them live with depression, relationship difficulties, low self-esteem, and all sorts of social and mental health issues.

If I could have chosen when to be born, I would not have been born before or during the Sudan civil war, which has destroyed our land and claimed the lives of many innocent South Sudanese people. I hate war and I hate seeing young people die in war. I was scared of guns, and my worst fears were realised when I heard gunfire coming from Mundari army barracks in Kajo-Keji. The barracks was fifteen or more miles away from our village, but the gunshots were loud enough to scare and traumatise me. It was as if they were fired from my backyard. The SPLA continuously raided the barracks where the Arabs were, until they overthrew the enemy and took over the barracks.

The first place raided by the SPLA in my neighbouring villages was my school, Logu primary school. One morning in the mid-1980s when I was in Year Two, a group of SPLA arrived during assembly. The teachers who were addressing the assembly saw a group of armed young men approaching the school, and they told the students not to panic. But most of the students ran for their lives. A few students, mostly in Years Five and Six, decided to stay behind and protect their headmaster and teachers as well as the young students. That morning, I did not see the SPLA, because I did not attend the assembly. I rarely attended assemblies because they were not disability friendly. They always took over an hour. I had no wheelchair and couldn't stand even for five minutes.

That beautiful morning, one of my friends who'd been at the assembly ran back to the classroom and told me to leave at once, because our school was being raided by the SPLA. I panicked and rushed out of the classroom, leaving my books behind. By this time, I was attending classes in a proper classroom, and I had books. As I wobbled quietly out of the classroom, I saw many students running for their lives. All the students, including my friend, ran the same way, but I left by a different route, as I was terrified that the SPLA might run after the students or fire bullets at them. Every time I heard people talking, or footsteps, or any noise, I would hide and wait until there was no more noise and then I would continue. When I was crossing a road, I would hide in a corner, look around, wait, look again, and then cross quickly. I saw no sign of the rebels or my schoolmates. I made it back home safely about two-

and-a-half hours later. Thank God I did not meet any man with a gun on my way home. I never went back to Logu primary school again. That was the end of my school life in Kajo-Keji, South Sudan.

A few days later, the SPLA started to come into the residential areas in the village. At first they only used one route to enter the village, which made it easy for the people to spot them from far away. So they would hide in the bushes and on the riverbanks before the rebels came to their houses. My family and our neighbours were always on the go to hide from the SPLA. Every day that passed, I was consumed with fear, as I didn't know if I would make it to the next day. Women with little babies were isolated and weren't allowed to take refuge together with the rest of the people in the bush because of the risk of the babies crying, coughing, and sneezing.

One day, the SPLA surprised the people by entering the village by a different route. Another time, a group of SPLA came to my home, and they took us by surprise. As a group of four SPLA approached our house, my mother, who saw them first, ran for her life, leaving me at home playing with my cousin Modong and another neighbour's daughter. I would have loved my mother to alert us before she took off, but she didn't have time. She hid in the bushes and came back later that day. The

SPLA came with chicken, which they cooked, and they forced me and my two friends to eat the chicken. I had no choice but to keep my mind off the guns around me, and I ate the chicken. This was the first time I'd come face to face with the SPLA. I was trembling, shaking, and sweating, but one SPLA in the group who spoke my language reassured me that they were not there to kill their own people. They had come to tell the people in the village not to migrate to other countries.

While two of the SPLA were cooking on my mother's firewood stove built of three stones outside the house, another two of them went into my house and found belongings packed in bags.

One of them came out and asked, "Who lives in this house?"

"I do," I said, trembling.

"Where are the rest of your family?" he asked.

"I live with my mother. She ran away when she saw you coming."

"Why did she run away?"

"She is scared of people with guns," I said.

"We are not bad people," he said. 'We are just ordinary people who have dedicated our lives to fight for our rights and for the rights of our people, and we do not want our people to run away from South Sudan," he said.

"You might be a good group of SPLA, but there are other people with guns who come to my village and kill people, rape women and young girls, and loot the village. People are terrified and they no longer want to live here," I said.

"Are you going to leave?" he asked.

"No, my mother is gone now, so I guess I will live here," I said. I really thought she had run away, not just left to hide for a while.

He looked at me, shook his head, spoke quietly to his friends, and they all laughed. I didn't know why the SPLA were laughing and what they were planning to do next. They spoke in South Sudanese–Bari language, which I could understand, as I am from the Bari speaking group, but they whispered to each other so I didn't hear what they said. My physical disability saved me from any kind of physical mistreatment and torture by the SPLA, as they believed that torturing or even meeting a person with a disability before going to battle brings bad luck to them. If one of them met a person with a disability, he would have to undergo some kind of cleansing ritual before he was allowed to go to the front line. Perhaps my mother knew that the SPLA wouldn't physically torture me because of my disability, and that's why she ran away without me.

As months went by, my village in South Sudan

began to look like a ghost town. My mum said that it was time to leave. My sisters were already in Abaya, Uganda. They didn't return. My mum and I were reunited with my sisters after we left Lomura village. The villagers migrated to neighbouring countries like Uganda, Kenya, and the Congo for refuge. At first, the people thought that if they went to their neighbouring countries for a few months, things might settle down, and they would be able to return to South Sudan. So they settled in what were called settlement zones close to the border of South Sudan. But as years went by and there was still no peace, the South Sudanese people, including those in my village, my family and I, decided to settle in refugee camps.

These were temporary zones for refugees in Uganda and in Kenya. Refugees living in the camps rely entirely on UNHCR relief (food, shelter, healthcare, water, and clothes) and they live in very hot tents provided by the UNHCR. They are like concentration camps where many people are packed into small areas. A lot of refugees die in these camps due to airborne diseases. Packing so many people in one small area means that if there is an outbreak of deadly contagious diseases, there will be little or no chance of survival.

The resettlement areas are more permanent. The Ugandan and the Kenyan government give refugees who are resettled their own piece of land, where they can grow their own food and build more permanent, grass-thatched houses. They may die there unless an opportunity comes up to be resettled in Western countries like Australia, Canada, the UK, USA, and other European countries.

Six

My Journey to Uganda as a Refugee

For me and my family and the people in my village, the journey to Uganda took many days, about a week on foot through the bush, where we survived on wild fruit and dirty water. Our neighbours and my sisters left for Uganda through the bush, leaving me, my mother, and Aunt Joggo alone in the village. At first, my mother refused to leave Lomura, because travelling on foot from South Sudan to Uganda, carrying me, was such a difficult task. I was seven years old, and quite a weight to carry so far. My aunt also decided to stay because she didn't want to leave her sister and niece alone in the village.

Change was something that my mother struggled with. She didn't want to leave her country, her village, and every beautiful thing in it. The thought of having to start from scratch in a foreign country terrified her.

Even though we were very poor in South Sudan, living in poverty in our village was far better than living in poverty in a refugee camp in a foreign country. But following the incident with the SPLA at my home that day, my mother finally decided that it was time to leave South Sudan. The village had already become a ghost town. Once a vibrant and noisy village filled with many interesting people who were full of life, Lomura had become quiet, lonely and terrifying. I could not even hear the beautiful singing birds. I guess they had migrated too. All the people except us had migrated and lived in different settlement areas in Uganda, not in one settlement area as a village, like they were used to in Kajo-Keji. Leaving Lomura as a refugee meant that I lost my village, school, family, and community support network.

Some people took food and water with them to eat and drink on the way, but when we left, my mother carried me and had to leave food and water behind. She carried me on her back all the way from Kajo-Keji to Uganda. We walked through the bush, and we slept on the dirt with nothing to cover ourselves. My cousin Wude, who left at the same time as my mum and me, took a big roasted sweet potato and two roasted maize cobs with her, and five litres of water. She shared her food with us, but when the food was finished, we ate wild guava, mangoes and other sweet wild fruits. We drank water from running rivers, wells, and even stagnant water in puddles in the bush. After many days' walk, I was reunited with my sisters, relatives, and a few people from our village in a place called Abaya at the border of South Sudan and Uganda.

Abaya was a jungle with no tents or houses. For a few weeks, we slept under a tree, where we were washed by the heavy Ugandan rains and were bitten by mosquitoes. There were also spiders, ants, snakes, and other creepy crawlies in the bush, plus wild animals, but we survived all of them. Weeks later, my uncle Wani built a small, one-room, grass-thatched house for the five of us to live in (me, my three sisters and my mother), and we enjoyed sleeping indoors for the first time in months. I thought that I could now relax, but I didn't know that Abaya jungle was a home to the Ugandan Juma Oris rebels.

Before long, the Juma Oris rebels started raiding, looting and killing the South Sudanese refugees in Abaya jungle, leaving some with serious injuries and others dead. The rebels were armed and supported by the Sudan government. One morning, when two rebels came to our house and threatened to shoot Uncle Wani and cut Angelina's head off in front of me, one of our closest neighbours ran to what they called the village centre, and beat a drum to alert the other refugees that there were rebels in the neighbourhood. The refugees responded straight away. They fought back, and many came to our house armed with bows and arrows, spears, machetes, and axes. One rebel who was threatening to shoot my uncle saw lots of armed men racing towards them. He alerted the other rebel, who was in my house searching for money, and they fled the scene in a hurry. The refugees chased the rebels until they crossed Abaya River. We left Abaya jungle for Lefori a few days later, where we lived until we were settled in Oliji Refugee Camp in Adjumani District, Northern Uganda.

Life became harder for me and my family in Lefori village, because there was no shelter, and no food or water. It was in Lefori that I became aware of the meaning of the word "racism". The Madi people in Lefori called the South Sudanese Kuku people *lowi bi ingwe*, which translates as foreigners with white ears. I don't even know what this means, I thought.

My family and all the other South Sudanese refugees in Lefori had to fight for water. If they won, they would get water, but if they lost, they would have no water. As if this was not enough, the insecurity was not over. Because Lefori was closer to Abaya jungle, the Juma

Oris rebels continued attacking the South Sudanese refugees, and I and my family often had to sleep in the bushes again.

While in Lefori, my family was given a piece of land by the Ugandan government to build a grass-thatched house, to cultivate and to grow our own food. Before we harvested our own produce in Lefori, my mother and sisters sometimes risked their lives to go back and forward to Kajo-Keji, South Sudan to collect food. During these trips, they came face to face with the SPLA on the way to and from South Sudan. They were physically and psychologically tortured by the SPLA when they were caught, as they were considered to be spies.

I was often left home alone in Lefori for days or weeks during these trips, wondering if I would ever see my family again. I went to the Madi people's well to fetch water and I roasted sweet potatoes for my meals. I also cooked porridge. Before my mum and sisters left, they would always cook food that lasted me for two to three days. All I had to do was to cook semolina to eat with the stew.

After a few months, my mother and sisters finally stopped going back and forth to South Sudan in search of food. We were able to harvest enough produce from the small piece of land we cultivated. The food included groundnuts (peanuts), maize, sweet potatoes, peas, beans, cassava, pumpkin, okra, onions, and other vegetables. Although we had enough food in Lefori, we didn't have money to buy meat, cooking salt, washing detergent, a bar of soap, or paraffin for lighting at night. But my mother was able to sell some of the produce in the local market in Lefori and in the big market in Moyo town, to earn money to purchase these necessary things. We used little lanterns with paraffin for light, and we gathered firewood for cooking.

Everybody in my house had a job to do. My job was to fetch water, wash clothes, do the dishes, and cook, while my mother and sisters went to the garden. My mother and sisters fetched water, firewood, cooked, and washed the clothes too, especially on weekends. I collected the water we used for drinking from a well. I was traumatised by verbal abuse and physical fights at the well. All the fights were over water. Women were often injured and bleeding. Mostly, the Madi women made the water dirty by jumping into the well or throwing things into it, so the South Sudanese women couldn't get their water.

I used containers like cooking pots and five litre jerrycans to carry water on my head. My mobility was made worse with the weight of the water on my head, which increased the number of falls I had, injuring my legs, arms and body, with cooking pots and jerrycans full of water falling on me. But at least, learning to cook and to do all the housework gave me the daily living skills that have enabled me to be more independent now. I am a good cook, and I am able to care and provide for my two beautiful daughters independently, with limited support.

Seven

Life in Ugandan Refugee camps

Because the Ugandan settlement policy states that all refugees and asylum seekers in Uganda must live in designated settlement areas, most of the South Sudanese refugees, including my family, lived in refugee camps or settlement areas. Most of these were located in Northern Uganda, including Nyumanzi 1 and 2, Keyo 1 and 2, Mongula, Maaji, Oliji, Ibakwe, and Belameling refugee camps. For some reasons, the South Sudanese refugees were at first settled on unfertile soil, and in the Ugandan Lord Resistance Army (LRA) territory in Northern Uganda, but were later resettled in fertile areas where they could grow their own food. Unfortunately, some of the areas where the South Sudanese refugees were later resettled, in Moyo and Lefori Districts, were areas occupied by the Ugandan Juma Oris rebels, and so the camps were constantly attacked by the rebels.

These areas were also accessible to the SPLA from South Sudan.

Like other South Sudanese refugees in the refugee camps in Uganda, I was physically and mentally affected by the ongoing attacks by the Lord Resistance Army (LRA) rebels under the leadership of Joseph Kony, and the Ugandan Juma Oris rebels in Northern Uganda. While the LRA claims to be fighting the Ugandan government, like the SPLA in South Sudan, the LRA has, in fact, brutally targeted the civilian population of Northern Uganda, killing men and raping women, looting villages, and abducting children, who were then forced to train as child soldiers, and mutilating innocent civilian bodies. As in South Sudan, some of these child soldiers were later sent back to their villages by Joseph Kony to torture and kill their own parents, their family members and relatives, and to burn down their own villages. As a result, thousands of Ugandans were displaced and were resettled in what the Ugandan government called "protected villages" in Northern Uganda. It was in these same unsafe areas that thousands of South Sudanese refugees, including my family, were resettled.

Several South Sudanese refugee camps in Adjumani, Uganda, were attacked a few times by the LRA, and the lack of careful analysis of the situation and of immediate and appropriate government response violated the fundamental human rights of the South Sudanese refugees. These attacks went on for so long that some refugees, including my relatives, kept returning to South Sudan.

Despite the intensity of the attacks, neither the United Nations High Commissioner for Refugees (UNHCR) nor the Ugandan government responded by closing the refugee camps in Adjumani district and by relocating the South Sudanese refugees to a safer location.

While additional army personnel were sent to defend some of the refugee camps in Northern Uganda, especially in Gulu and Adjumani Districts, there were no army personnel sent to Palorinya and Lefori refugee camps where majority of the South Sudanese refugees were resettled. Although the lives of the South Sudanese refugees in the camps that were attacked by the LRA were in danger, the government of Uganda did nothing to stop the attacks, and failed to relocate the refugees to safer areas. The majority of the displaced South Sudanese refugees were later resettled in other refugee camps in Northern Uganda, but the Ugandan government decided to move the remaining South Sudanese refugees, including my family, back to the extreme end of Northern Uganda; this time to different refugee camps in Moyo and Lefori districts, close to the border of South Sudan and Uganda. The refugee camps in Moyo district in Uganda, including Ibakwe and Belameling, where we were resettled, were located in Juma Oris rebel territory. So the refugees were being resettled in what the UNHCR called "a war zone," where their lives were again placed at risk. The fact that the majority of the refugees in the displaced refugee camps were South Sudanese refugees and were resettled close to the border of Uganda and South Sudan violated international law. Resettling the refugees in brutal war zones in Uganda was a clear breach of the refugee international law, as explained in the UNHCR Refugee Protection: A Guide to International Law.

As mentioned, besides the Lord Resistance Army in Uganda, there was another group of Ugandan rebels led by Juma Oris, who were supported by the Sudan government. This group of Ugandan rebels constantly attacked Ibakwe, Belameling, and other refugee camps in and around the Palorinya area in Moyo District, Northern Uganda, and they set refugees' houses ablaze. During these attacks, some of the refugees were burnt alive in their own houses by the rebels. These brutal acts of burning South Sudanese refugees, especially men, in their houses, were witnessed by family members, including children. Most of the South Sudanese children and men also witnessed their mothers, wives, sisters and other female relatives being raped by the rebels in the refugee camps in their presence. Every time the rebels attacked the refugee camps, a group of three to four rebels would seize a family and would force every member of the family to sit, kneel or stand and watch their female relatives, wives, daughters, aunties and sisters being raped by the rebels. They could do nothing to stop the rape from taking place, as guns were held to their heads and knives or machetes were held to their throats.

These unspeakable rebel acts left permanent emotional scars in the victims, the children, and their families. The screaming and the cries for help of the rape victims is what the children who witnessed the rape will have to live with for the rest of their lives. Nightmares and all sorts of ongoing mental health issues are the burden these South Sudanese children have to bear, both in the refugee camps and in the Western world. Many of the South Sudanese refugee survivors of rape, torture and death in Moyo refugee camps fled the camps and once again resettled in Adjumani refugee camps, which were not safe, but others, including my relatives, decided to return to their original home areas in South

Sudan. But most of those who had returned to South Sudan returned and resettled in the refugee camps in Uganda once again, because they were starving back home in South Sudan.

You are probably asking yourselves the question, what really goes on in Ugandan refugee camps? Well, come with me and I will tell you all about what really happened in the three Ugandan refugee camps that I lived in. After living in Lefori village for three years, like other South Sudanese refugees seeking refugee status in Uganda, my mother and sisters went to the United Nations High Commissioner for Refugees office in Pakele, Adjumani District, in Northern Uganda, to be registered as refugees. I was left in Lefori village on my own once again. I had grown taller, bigger, and heavier, so my mother was no longer able to carry me on her back to the UNHCR office in Adjumani, which was more than forty-five miles away from Lefori village. There was no transport from Lefori village to the UNHCR office in Adjumani, so my family had to walk there. My mother and sisters spent more than a week in Adjumani waiting to be registered as refugees, and following their registration they were resettled in Oliji refugee camp in Adjumani district. I was thrilled to join my mother and sisters in the refugee camp two weeks after they were registered as refugees. My mother sent a relative with a bicycle to come and collect me from Lefori and take me to the camp. The bicycle was borrowed from someone in the camp.

Eight
Life in Oliji Refugee Camp

Resettling in Oliji refugee camp meant that once more, we had to leave our food and shelter behind in Lefori village, which made our lives very precarious. Although we were provided with a tent by the UNHCR office, and managed to set it up, the tent was worse than the grass-thatched house we had left behind in Lefori village, as it was boiling hot. After we had endured many hot days and nights in the tent, my uncle and neighbours helped us build another grass-thatched house in the camp. Like any other refugee camps, life in Oliji refugee camp was very hard. We lacked food, medication, and clean water, and suffered unhygienic, wretched living conditions in inadequate shelter. Wild weather was the order of the day. The weather was very hot and dry, with heavy winds and sand twisters, which covered the whole camp in red sand and dust on most evenings.

The winds blew roofs, cooking pots, cooked food, and clothes away, and damaged the tents and grass-thatched houses. Because there were no good materials for building strong houses that could withstand such harsh weather conditions, we spent most of our time rebuilding houses, only to see them blown away again by the heavy winds and sand twisters. Most of the refugees in Oliji camp had no money to buy food, and had to survive on only one meal per day. Some, including my family, went for days without food.

The entire camp of about two million or more South Sudanese refugees had only three boreholes. A family would have to queue for days or weeks to collect only twenty litres of water. Many of us, especially the women, could only dream of having a bath. The boreholes were prone to breaking down most of the time due to over-pumping.

As if the lack of water was not enough, tribal war broke out, with refugees fighting each other over the water. The weak, unlucky ones lost their lives at the boreholes.

"I thought that I had left fighting over water back in Lefori village. But I was wrong. There is even more fighting over water here. At least in Lefori village, nobody was killed at the well," I complained to my family. But wait; there was more tribal war to come.

This time, the tribal war was not related to lack of water, but to the Sudan civil war.

I asked myself, what have we got ourselves into? Will this violence ever stop? As if the fighting over water in Oliji refugee camp was not enough, cultural and political war broke out in Oliji refugee camp. The South Sudanese refugees blamed each other for the Sudan Civil war. Ex SPLA soldiers who escaped the civil war and resettled in Oliji refugee camp as refugees were the main targets in the refugee camp. The Arabs who had also migrated to Oliji refugee camp for business purposes were also the targets of the war.

One beautiful afternoon, some of the South Sudanese refugees in the camp combined forces and seized the Arab residential and business areas, and set the whole area on fire. According to those involved in the fight, the war was a revenge for what the Arabs did to the South Sudanese people in Sudan. Many people were killed during this war, and others sustained serious injuries. Although not all South Sudanese refugees were involved in the physical fight at the Arab areas that afternoon, onlookers participated in looting the Arab businesses in and around the war zone. Kitchen knives, sticks, and farm tools, as well as blows and guns, were used as weapons. Some of the Arabs ran for their lives, but others fought back and shot many South

Sudanese refugees who were involved in the fight that afternoon. Innocent onlookers were also killed.

Oh my God, when am I ever going to stop witnessing war? I said to myself. War, war, war! Why war? I asked. I am sick and tired of war and witnessing young people die in war, I continued, while shedding tears. I want PEACE, PEACE, and PEACE. Despite the fact that the South Sudanese refugees in Oliji refugee camp blamed and hated each other for the Sudan civil war, on this particular day, they all combined forces to fight their common enemy, the Arabs. A few days later, the Arabs who had survived the fight that afternoon left Oliji refugee camp, and they went back to where they came from. At least in Lefori village, life was good at last. We had developed a good relationship with the Madi people in Lefori, and water and food were no longer an issue for us. Whereas in Oliji refugee camp, there was no piece of land to cultivate and grow food on. All we could do was to wait for the UNHCR office in Adjumani district to provide us with food—a few kilos of maize flour, dry beans, rice, cooking oil and salt, and a bar of soap for washing, supplied just once a month—but the supply was not enough to last for two weeks, let alone a month.

Deadly airborne, highly contagious diseases such as cholera, measles, chicken pox, meningitis, diarrhoea, and malaria, broke out and claimed the lives of many South Sudanese refugees. I am so blessed to have survived these diseases. For a long time, I was scared of going to sleep, as I was always woken up in the middle of the night by people screaming, crying and wailing over the death of their loved ones. You would go to sleep and by the time you woke up, you would find that six or more South Sudanese refugees had died near you because of these diseases. When I was twelve, my sister Edith died in 1992 in Mulago Hospital, Moyo, in Northern Uganda, after contracting liver disease in Oliji refugee camp.

For so long before I came to Australia, I suffered from nightmares. But I have had professional help here to help me deal with the trauma that I experienced in the refugee camps and in my childhood and now, I have no issues going to sleep. Despite all that happened in Oliji refugee camp, the South Sudanese refugees, including my family, embraced the life style, and moved on with our lives as best we could, as the camp had become our home. Refugee men, especially, established small retail shops, and their businesses flourished. The camp was a good place for business, but it was not good for agriculture because of its wild weather. The men travelled long distances to sell some of the food provided by the UNCHR in the big markets in Adjumani and Moyo, and they bought clothes and other goods cheaply to sell in the refugee camp. They added a few shillings to every item they sold to get big profits, which they then used to buy more stock. The women used some of their UNCHR food (maize) to brew alcohol and sell it to get money, which they also used to buy stock for their shops.

All the South Sudanese tribes that were in Oliji refugee camp maintained their culture and traditions, organising traditional dances such as *Kore, Bula, Mure,* and singing traditional songs. But other refugees, especially the young ones who intermarried and integrated into other South Sudanese cultures, diluted their original culture. They took part in disco dancing and other dances the Kuku people call *ayije* and *adungu.* Marriage and child-naming ceremonies were encouraged and maintained in the refugee camp, and Christmas, New Year and Easter were celebrated. Some South Sudanese refugees became Church ministers (pastors, preachers, evangelists and Church elders).

When I was ten or eleven years old, I joined the Church choir, which enabled me to receive the biggest blessing of my life, changing my life forever—education. This was just the beginning of good things to happen in my life. One Sunday morning, an Italian Catholic Priest called Father Mario came to my Church and offered to pay my school fees. A month later, I moved to live in Moyo Catholic Mission with Father Mario, where I went to school, and at Senior Four level, I completed the Uganda Certificate of Education under a scholarship from the Catholic Church. Senior Four Certificate of Education in Uganda is equivalent to Year Ten Certificate in Australia.

Unfortunately, Father Mario became ill and was flown back to Italy. That was the last time I heard of Father Mario. I am not sure if he is still alive or if he is dead. I would like to know what happened to Father Mario, and if he is dead, where he is buried.

Some South Sudanese refugees became teachers, but others stayed at home doing nothing, and causing a lot of trouble with their criminal behaviour, including looting, stealing, shop lifting, fighting, and under-age sex. Before I moved to study in Moyo Girls Primary School in Northern Uganda, I attended school in the refugee camp in a primary school near my home. Living in the refugee camp was like living in a dark hole where there was no light, no fresh air to breathe, and no hope for the future. In refugee camps, people are cut off from the world and suffer many ongoing mental health issues.

A few months after resettling in Oliji refugee camp, my sister Angelina left the camp for Moyo Catholic

Mission to look for work, and she was lucky to find employment as a cook and housekeeper for Father Mario and his priest colleagues in the mission. About four months later in 1990, I too went to live in the same Catholic mission with my sister, and I went to Moyo Girls Primary school under the scholarship of the Catholic Church in Moyo. I was in Year Five in Primary school when I joined Moyo Girls Primary School in 1990.

Nine

Inside Ibakwe refugee camp

Three years after I went to live in Moyo Catholic Mission and study at Moyo Girls Primary School, my mother, Margaret, and my sister, Selina, were finally resettled in a fertile area where they were able to grow their own food. This refugee camp was called Ibakwe refugee camp in Moyo District near River Nile. But their life in Ibakwe refugee camp became a real nightmare, as the forest, which was transformed into the camp, was a home to the Ugandan rebels led by Juma Oris. The heavy rains flooded the camp, making life very difficult in such harsh and poor living conditions. As mentioned earlier, Ibakwe refugee camp was also accessible to the SPLA from South Sudan. The SPLA constantly raided the camp, looking for ex-SPLA soldiers who had resettled as refugees to be returned to South Sudan to continue fighting the Arabs. Ibakwe refugee camp and

Belameling refugee camp, plus other camps around the Palorinya area, were continuously attacked by the Juma Oris rebels and the SPLA. Houses and the UNHCR offices in these camps, including medical facilities, were looted and burnt down, leaving refugees with no medication. Many security men who guarded the medical centres and the UNCHR offices in the camps, as well as staff, were killed during these raids.

One Sunday afternoon, after my mother and I had just returned from the Church, we heard intense ongoing shooting that lasted for about an hour. The Juma Oris rebels had attacked the staff and looted the UNHCR office. Many staff and rebels were killed that afternoon. Thank goodness they didn't set the UNHCR office on fire; if they had, the whole of Ibakwe refugee camp would have been engulfed with fire. It was a very hot, dry and windy afternoon. All the refugees in Ibakwe refugee camp ran and hid at the mountain that was near the camp. My mother asked me to go and hide at the mountain with the rest of the refugees, but she refused to run. She said that she was tired of running. She also said that she didn't have a reason to run anymore, now that her children are all grown up. I didn't want to run and hide in the bushes either, because to me, running to the mountain was pointless, given that the Juma Oris rebels lived in the mountains. This time, I was ready to face whatever was coming my way that afternoon; but God protected us. The refugee camp went quiet for the whole afternoon and night. The refugees returned to the camp the following morning. An hour after the gunfire, everything went quiet, and thank God, the rebels didn't go to the residential areas in the refugee camp. My mother and I survived the whole ordeal alone in the camp, terrified, not knowing where the gunshots were going to come from next, but we were reunited with all the other refugees in the camp the following day.

A few months after resettling in Ibakwe refugee camp, Selina, who was about sixteen at the time, decided that she has had enough of the tough refugee life, so she went to live in Moyo town in Northern Uganda, with the hope of finding a job as a housekeeper. Before she got a job, she met and married the father of her kids, leaving our mother to live on her own in the refugee camp.

I could only imagine how terrifying living alone must have been for my mother. My mother was from a big family, and she had six children. All of a sudden, she was left on her own without any family, and without any support. Although there were other refugees near my mother whom she had become friends with, living without her children was difficult for her. She started to skip cooking and having meals. This time she had plenty of food from her garden, and the borehole was near her house, but she wasn't happy, because she had no children to share her food with. Only when I visited her and stayed with her for a week would she cook and eat. I visited my mother during school holidays, but that was only once in three months. Angelina also visited my mother, but as she was married with two little children, these visits were irregular.

Ibakwe refugee camp had more than one borehole close to my mother, which meant that clean drinking water was no longer a problem. Despite the fact that there was plenty of food, clean water, appropriate shelter, and medication in Ibakwe refugee camp, my mother and other South Sudanese refugees in the camp did not enjoy staying in the camp, due to the ongoing attacks by the rebels and the SPLA.

I went to Metu Secondary School after completing Year Seven at Moyo Girls Primary school. I studied Senior Level One to Four, which is equivalent to year Seven, Eight, Nine and Ten in primary school in Australia, and I went to Advanced Secondary Levels Five and Six in Bombo Secondary School. The advanced level is called A Level in Uganda, and it is equivalent to Years Eleven and Twelve in Australia.

When my sister, Angelina, got married, and after

she had her first child, I went to live with her to help her with babysitting duties and housework. My sister lived near Moyo Catholic Mission. I was in boarding school in Metu, and helped her during school holidays. After Father Mario was flown back to Italy following his illness, I was left with nobody to pay my school fees. However, I am so grateful that Angelina's husband, Dickson, was able to pay my school fees in Bombo Secondary School in my Advance Secondary Levels Five and Six.

When I went to live with my sister, Father Mario stopped giving me pocket money, as he thought that my sister and her husband would take care of my school requirements, including pocket money and everything else. This meant that I had to stay at school during short school breaks and public holiday weekends, because I didn't have money to go back home for two to three days and then back to school.

There were times in Metu Secondary School when I had to stay in the hostel and skip classes, because I had my period and had no pads to wear. I went back to attend classes when I was dry. Before I left home for school at the beginning of every term, my sister bought me a packet with twelve pads in it, which was not enough to last for the whole term of three months. I didn't even have enough money to buy paraffin for lighting and reading at night. There was, however, a nun at Metu Secondary School who helped me with paraffin and a bar of soap a few times. I also went to Metu Seminary a few times to ask for money from one of the South Sudanese priests there and from the Bishop himself, to help me buy pads, nickers, paraffin and a bar of soap after I run out of the things I brought from home.

Bombo Secondary School, where I did Levels Five and Six, had electricity, and it had student services to help students from very poor families with the necessary school items they needed to help them stay at school and concentrate on their studies. Bombo Secondary School provided me with one kilogram of sugar and one-and-a-half bars of soap every term. There was also a female teacher for female students to talk to, and a male teacher for male students from very poor families, to talk to when we needed to. It was the school counsellor's responsibility to refer students like me to the school shop to collect the items they needed. Not every student in the school was eligible to receive assistance from the school shop, as the school policy stated that students could only receive items they needed from the shop after presenting a referral letter from the teacher counsellors. Those teachers were like student counsellors in Australia.

When I was in Senior Five, and for the first half

of my Senior Six, I had two uniform skirts and two uniform shirts, and one good dress to use for Church at school on Sundays. I stayed in my school uniform most of the time, even after school and on Saturdays, because I had no other clothes to change into. Some of the students from rich families at Bombo Secondary School gave me some clothes to wear and food to eat. But I only used the clothes at school. I was afraid of taking the clothes home, because I didn't want to be accused of stealing the clothes or prostituting myself to get money for the clothes. Moreover, I didn't want to be stopped from going back to Bombo Secondary School, so I kept all the assistance I received from the school as secret. In saying that, after I completed my A level studies, I took one outfit home which was given to me by the Pastor's wife from the Church near the school where I attended Church services at Bombo.

Ten

Life in Kampala City

After my Advanced Secondary School in Bombo, I stayed home for a year without going to university or college in Uganda because I didn't have any money. Robert, a South Sudanese man I met at Church, was kind enough to give me money to start a retail shop so I could earn money to pay for my school fees. He was compassionate; he saw something in me that nobody else saw, and he trusted me with his hard-earned money. The plan was for me to open the business, manage it, and give him the money I got from selling the items at the shop, and he would pay my wages at the end of every month until he got back the money he had invested in starting the shop. He would only take from the profits the money that he had invested in starting the business. So I started the retail shop business; it would then be up to me to continue with the business, or to do something else after that.

After a few months, the business was flourishing, and Robert and I started making plans for me to go to college; we talked about what college I wanted to go to, and what I was going to study. Robert was going to pay my school fees at college with money from his teaching job, and he wanted me to have the shop to help me set up for living. Robert was happy with the work I did in managing the shop. At this time, I had already paid back the money he borrowed to me for the shop.

I was happy, but before long, my family started making allegations that Robert was sleeping with me and that he was using me. Robert and I were not in any relationship. My family could not understand the kindness he had shown me and my family, so they asked him to take his shop and money away from me and to leave me alone. My family thought that Robert was interested in me sexually, and that that was why he didn't have issues with giving his money to me. Robert tried to reason with them, but things became nasty, so he decided to take back the shop, and he gave it to his sister. A week later, my brother in-law, Dickson, gave me money to start a similar retail shop like the one I had with Robert, to enable me pay my school fees. I started the shop and my sister took over a few months later. That was the last time I worked in the shop. I wasn't allowed to work in the shop anymore.

As if the hard life as a refugee, my strict upbringing, and my disability was not enough, I was physically attacked in December 1999 and was left with a significant head injury. Three weeks before Christmas, three men broke into my sister's house in Kampala. Three men whom I knew from my sister's shop forced their way into my sister' house. It was 5:00 a.m. when I heard a big bang on the door, and the next thing I saw was a big rock landing on the floor inside the house near the door. The big rock landed a few centimetres away from Poni's legs. Poni was a visiting family relative who slept in the lounge with me that night. I slept on the couch and Poni slept on a mattress on the floor. The big rock woke me up. I sat on the couch and I saw the door wide open. I panicked and shouted, "Poni wake up, we are in danger!" but she was in a very deep sleep, unaware of what was happening. Our neighbours heard the loud bang of the rock, but Poni didn't hear it. Our next door neighbour had her door locked from the outside by the three men before they broke into my sister's house.

Two of the men struck Poni on the head several times with two big logs, so hard that Poni stopped breathing. I recognised one of the men as a customer from my sister's shop, and I called out to him, "Tom, why … why are you beating Poni? What has she done to you people?" But Tom was quiet. The next thing I knew, there was a big bang on my head. I shouted in pain. Rob, Tom's friend, who was standing by the door, struck my head with a metal bar, and cracked my forehead open. Blood splashed around me.

I believe Rob was going to kill me to shut me up, so I couldn't tell the story about who broke into my sister's house, but I kept praying, calling out the name of Jesus while he kept striking my head, and God protected me. I should have kept my mouth shut the minute I saw Tom and his friends, but I wasn't going to lie there and do nothing while they killed Poni. Many people in situations like this would freeze or go into a shock mode, but I was vocal, and I was determined to protect my sister's house with everyone in it. Angelina and Selina were awake in the bedroom and they heard everything, but they didn't come out of the bedroom.

As I continued praying, with blood splashing everywhere and Rob still hitting my head, Tom and his friends panicked, and they fled the house with my sister's television, leaving me in a pool of blood. I was convinced that Tom and his friends were not burglars but were there to kill me, as they only took the TV and left the remote. The TV remote was on top of the TV, but they placed it on top of the DVD player, and they left. Why would they take a TV without the remote, and why would they not take the DVD player if they were burglars? DVD players were very expensive in Uganda at the time, and not everyone could afford them. Because Tom and his friends did not ask for money, and Poni and I were the only people attacked in the house, I believe that the motive for this attack was not robbery, but I cannot understand or explain the reason why the attack took place.

Perhaps jealousy was the motive, or somebody paid them to kill me. Maybe they thought that I was the one sleeping on the floor and they thought that they were beating me on the head instead of Poni. I used to sleep on the floor before Poni visited us. I think that Tom and his friends might have been informed that I would be the only person sleeping on the lounge floor; that's why two of them struck Poni on the head and one of them stood by the door waiting. They didn't even look around to see if there was somebody else in the room.

At first, I didn't know that I was injured or that I was losing a lot of blood, so I got off the couch to check if Poni was breathing, but I stumbled and I fell back on the couch. I felt lightheaded, and I could smell something, so I lowered my head and looked at the floor, and I noticed that there was liquid pouring out of my head. I touched my forehead and felt my fingers were wet. I tried to get up from the couch again to turn the light on and see what was going on, but I fell back onto the couch and collapsed. I called out for help, but after Tom and his friends had left, it took five minutes for Angelina and Selina to come out of the bedroom. It was a one-bedroom house. Few weeks later, we moved into another house. This time it was a three bedroom house.

I was alert, but very weak and thirsty. Poni was non-responsive. When Selina and Angelina finally came out of the bedroom, they turned the light on, and I heard some screaming and wailing. My blood had splashed all over the room, including on the walls, on the floor, on the couch, and on Poni. My sisters were standing in my pool of blood. I didn't know whether my sisters were crying because there was a lot of blood on the floor and on the wall, or because there were two bodies on the floor. Blood was still gushing out of my forehead and I would later need a blood transfusion to keep me alive. My mind was telling me to get up and help Poni, so I tried to get up again, but Selina told me not to move because of the blood pouring out of my head. Angelina had run out of the house to ask for help from the neighbours.

Our closest neighbour, Jane, was a nurse, so she came in to help me and Poni and she provided first aid.

The next thing I knew, a taxi was parked in front of our house, and we were loaded into the taxi. Our neighbour took us to the hospital where she worked at the time. I was so thirsty, and I wanted to drink some water but Jane refused to give me water to drink. She said that the water would kill me. Jane put some pressure and a bandage on my head to stop the bleeding. I passed out from the blood loss. But I regained consciousness shortly after. I went in and out of consciousness many times, but I was stable at the hospital. The doctors at the hospital said that I had a five-centimetre deep and five-centimetre long open wound on my forehead. They said that I was lucky to survive, as the metal had cut a major artery in my head.

The wound was stitched, and I was discharged from the hospital later that day. The doctors wanted to keep me at the hospital for observation and monitoring, but we didn't have money to keep both me and Poni in the hospital. Poni's situation was more severe than mine, because she had internal injuries, so she had to stay in the hospital. On the way to the hospital, Poni vomited blood and that was not a good sign, but she was discharged from the hospital and she recovered well. No brain injury, thank goodness.

God protected me, and I survived my head and arm injury. I protected my head with my arms when

Rob was hitting my head with the metal and my right arm was wounded. For three months, my head wasn't working properly, but I recovered well. When I went to sleep every night and woke up in the night to go to the toilet, I did not remember where the door was or where I was. I currently suffer from dizziness on and off, which I think might be related to the head injury I sustained in Kampala, Uganda. Poni also recovered well.

I joined Makerere Institute of Professionals four months later, and I graduated with a Diploma in Social Work in 2001. I had school fees from my sister's shop to complete my social work diploma, but I didn't have money for transport and food in my second year of my social work studies, so I used the skills I learnt from the women in Lomura village to make table cloths and sell them. I also dressed neighbours' hair to get a little money. My sister told me that she could no longer afford to pay my school fees and give me money for food and transport at the same time. I was not living in a hostel, but travelled from home to the college every day.

When I was in my first year of social work studies, my neighbour Sam, who was a driver for one of the ministers in parliament in Uganda, gave me a lift from home to the city every morning in the minister's car! When he dropped me off at the city, I caught a connecting bus from the city to the college; his assistance helped me save some money from transport for food.

One morning, half way through my first year of college, I met a Ugandan man called Sam on my way to the bus stop. A car passed me by and pulled over on the side of the road ahead of me. The driver got out of his car, opened the passenger door, and asked me to get in.

"Hello, how are you?" said Sam.

"Fine, thank you; how are you? What can I do for you?" I asked.

"Get in and give me the honour of transporting you to where you are going," said Sam.

Wow, nobody had ever said this to me before. "Thank you for the offer, but no thank you; I won't get into your car," I said.

"I am going the same direction as you, so please get in the car and let me give you a lift," said Sam.

"No, I do not get into strangers' cars," I said.

Sam laughed, and said, "I am not a stranger. I am a neighbour of yours; I see you walk this way every morning. Let me help you today, please."

"No, I know my way to where I am going and I will get there by myself," I said.

"Drop the pride; we all need help at some point. Get in the car and let me give you a lift," Sam insisted.

"Do not be scared of me. I am a good man who just wants to help you, so please get in the car," he added.

"What does a bad man look like?" I asked, and I walked way.

"Come on, stop wasting time. I am rushing to work and I just want to give you a lift, since I am heading the same direction as you."

"No, I will walk, thank you," I said, and I continued walking. Sam got into his car and drove off, but he again pulled over a few metres ahead of me, and he reversed his car towards me and got out of the car again.

"Are you going to school or not?" He asked.

"Yes, but why it is any of your business?"

"Get in the car please, and let me give you a lift," said Sam.

"You do not give up, do you?" I asked.

"No, only when you are around," he said, and he laughed.

I laughed, and I asked, "Why me?"

"Because you are so special I guess," said Sam.

For some reasons, Sam managed to convince me, and I willingly entered his car. He took me to the college and for the first time, I was early and I got to save that transport money for food.

On the way to the college, Sam told me his life story, and I was shocked. "I am from a very poor peasant family where education is not an option, but I managed to complete the Ugandan Certificate of Education through hard work," he said. "I didn't continue with further education due to lack of money!" he added. "After all that I have been through, I am very lucky to have been employed as a minister's driver", he said. "I like and admire young people like you who go to school", said Sam. Sam told me not to give up in life, no matter what, and he encouraged me to read hard and help people in the world in the future, especially Ugandans. He said that the car he was driving was not his own, but if I studied hard, I would buy and drive my own car, and hopefully one day, he would get to ride in my car.

Sam's prophecy came to pass in part, because I now drive my own car. At first, I was scared of being kidnapped by Sam, but I discovered that Sam and I had so many things in common, related to our childhoods. He continued driving me to the college, and he started picking me up from home instead of me waiting for him on the road.

Agreeing to Sam picking me up from home was a big mistake, as my lifts with him ended unexpectedly after a relative confronted him and things were said to him. Sam and I had made an agreement before that he would only pick me up from the road and nobody from my family was to know that he was driving me to the college, but one day Sam picked me up from home. The last time Sam dropped me at college, he picked me up from home and he told me that a family member of mine had spoken to him, and because of that, he could not keep driving me to college anymore. He didn't tell me who from my family spoke to him and what was said to him. I felt guilty that I had put Sam in such a situation. I still communicate with Sam, and he is very happy to know that I am in Australia, renting my own place and driving my own car.

The first day I entered Sam's car, I said to myself, what a fortune! Who am I to be driven in a minister's car when I do not even have a relative who is a politician, a minister, or a member of parliament? Not knowing that I would become a politician myself and would one day run for Parliament in Australia, I thought that Sam was crazy to even allow me to ride in the minister's car. But God was actually communicating to me through Sam.

Surely miracles do happen, and this is my miracle, I said to myself. I needed transport to the college because of my mobility impairment, and there, I got it. I do believe that God works in mysterious ways and he makes a way where there seems to be no way. Sam's wife Hannah, who became my friend later, was okay with Sam helping me, but when my family found out, they stopped him.

My physical disability and mobility impairment made walking to and from the bus stop to the college very difficult for me. I walked for thirty minutes from home to the bus stop to catch a bus to the city, and then I caught another bus from the city to the college. Muddy roads during rainy season made the road conditions very difficult for me. I skipped classes on wet, muddy, rainy days. The help from Sam was my saving grace. Despite all that happened to me, my determination helped me graduate from college with a Social Work Diploma.

When I had the time and if there was no one in the house, I used the kitchen or the lounge in my sister's house for my studies during my college years, because I didn't have a bedroom to use for my studies. Most of the time, I didn't study if the house was busy. In my final year of college in Uganda, things were very hard for me, but at least I had time to study. This time, my sister had decided to cook at the shop and she fed her children at the shop after picking them up from school. She didn't bring any food home after work so I ate at the neighbours' houses sometimes. Other times, I used my transport money for food. I also collected vegetables from my neighbours' gardens and cooked in my sister's house. There was an empty spare bedroom where I was living at the time, but I wasn't allowed to use the spare bedroom. Because I was sleeping on the couch in the living room, I was the first person to get up every morning to make room for everyone, and I was the last person to go to sleep after everyone had gone to bed.

In early 2002, after I completed my social work diploma studies, I approached the police in Kampala, Uganda with the aim of obtaining city refugee status and being resettled in Kyangwali refugee camp. During my interview with the police, I told the police that I was a South Sudanese refugee woman who was seeking asylum in Uganda. I told them that I tried to live a normal life in Kampala city like any other Ugandan citizen, but things were not going well with me in Kampala due to lack of food, shelter, and discrimination in the Ugandan employment sector. Before this time, I could not identify myself as a South Sudanese refugee to any Ugandan, because of the high level of racism and discrimination that prevailed in Uganda at the time. It was also difficult to get a job in Uganda if one identified as a South Sudanese Refugee.

The police took time to listen to my story, and they sent me with a letter to the Interaid office, which was close to the police station; here, I attended a number of interviews. The Interaid office in Kampala, Uganda was a processing centre in the city for refugees and asylum seekers who were to be resettled in the city or in a refugee camp in Uganda, with the hope of further resettlement in the Western World. After the interview with the police and further interviews with the Interaid office, I was finally referred to the UNHCR office in Kololo, Kampala, Uganda, to be processed for resettlement in Kyangwali refugee camp. I couldn't be happier, because I knew then that if I was successful and I got resettled in Kyangwali refugee camp, there would be a seventy-five percent chance of me being resettled in the Western world.

Being referred by the police to the Interaid office and then to the UNHCR office in Kampala, Uganda, was a tough, but quick way of being granted city refugee status in Kampala city. Usually for someone to be referred to the Interaid and to the UNHCR office in Kampala by the police, the person has to pay a huge amount of money to the police before the process can even begin. But because I didn't have money, I obtained a support letter from the head of Makerere Institute of Professionals where I completed my Social Work Diploma. The Head of the College knew my situation very well and he was more than happy to provide me with a support letter to ensure that I received the support that I needed. The support letter explained in detail the length of time I had spent in Uganda, the studies I had undertaken in Uganda, and the hardships I was experiencing in Uganda as a refugee. Six months after attending a series of interviews in three different offices in Kampala, Uganda, I was successfully resettled in Kyangwali refugee camp in Western Uganda.

Many people queued every day at Interaid and at the UNHCR office in Kampala, Uganda, including those who had paid a huge amount of money, but most of them were not successful in obtaining city refugee status, let alone in being resettled. God's favour was upon my life. Because I didn't have a phone for people to call me, I went to the Interaid office once every two days to check the progress of my case.

The last time I went there, I was told that I would be travelling to Kyangwali refugee camp in seven days' time. They told me the date, the time, and where to go to wait for the UNCHR car to take me to the bus station. They gave me money for food and transport. I dropped down on my knees, I prayed, thanking God, and I cried. A few minutes later I left the Interaid office still crying. Some refugees who saw me crying thought that I failed my interview, but I was crying tears of joy.

I went back to my sister's house and I told her that I was going to Kyangwali refugee camp in seven days' time. She wasn't happy that I was leaving and going far away, but I was ready to take care of myself and to be alone without bothering anybody. I washed my clothes the following day and packed my things, ready to leave my sister's house, even though it was not yet time to leave. I couldn't wait for the seven days to pass. I wasn't scared that I was going far away, to a place I didn't know, to live there by myself. I wasn't worried at all about whether I would get accommodation, water, and or food in the camp, or whether I would meet anyone I know there. I was ready to go because I felt like I was a burden to all those around me. It was high time I started taking care of myself, I thought to myself.

Eleven

Life in Kyangwali Refugee Camp

The travelling date arrived, and I hired a taxi to take me to the Interaid office. I was able to afford a taxi this time because the Interaid office had given me money for food and transport. My two neighbours also gave me money and food to help me on the way. It was 4:00 p.m. when the Interaid staff loaded my things and me onto a big bus that was to take me to Hoima town. I was in the company of other successful refugees and two Interaid staff, who were there to make sure that we got to Kyangwali refugee camp. In the past, some rich Ugandan people had gone to the Interaid office and obtained city refugee status, but never went to the refugee camp they were asked to go to. Instead, they applied to be resettled in the Western world from Kampala city, and some of them were resettled in Australia as South Sudanese refugees. By this time, the Interaid staff were aware of what was going on, so they had to accompany us to the camp to make sure we arrived there.

We arrived at Hoima at 6:00 p.m., and we caught another bus to Kyangwali refugee camp from Hoima at 9:30 p.m. Because I was the youngest in the group, all the other refugees made sure I was well taken care of. They used the money given to them by Interaid to buy food and water for me. They also took good care of my luggage. The Interaid staff paid for our transport from Kampala to Hoima and on to Kyangwali refugee camp. They also gave us spending money to help us until we received assistance from the camp authority. We arrived at Kyangwali refugee camp at 1:00 a.m., and we were taken to the police station in the camp, where we were detained for the remainder of the night. The following day, we were taken to the UNHCR office in the refugee camp, where we were processed and then released to the community.

I was lucky to be provided with suitable accommodation in a home of a South Sudanese woman called Annette, whom I knew in Kampala through my sister. I was also lucky to receive emotional and physical support from other South Sudanese families in the refugee camp in terms of collecting water for me, doing my grocery shopping, and someone to talk to if I needed it.

Kyangwali refugee camp was different from Oliji and Ibakwe refugee camps, in the sense that Kyangwali refugee camp was a centre for asylum seekers who were supposed to be resettled in the western world. The other refugee camps in Uganda were only to resettle refugees in Uganda, to live and die there. Most of the refugees in Kyangwali refugee camp were people from big cities, including Juba and Yei in South Sudan, and Khartoum in Northern Sudan and Kampala in Uganda. Some of these refugees in Kyangwali refugee camp were people who had attained a certain level of education in their countries of origin. Whereas Oliji, Ibakwe, and Belameling were refugee camps for South Sudanese refugees only, Kyangwali was a refugee camp for many African refugees including the Sudanese and the Congolese.

Being a human rights social worker who believes in a fair go for refugees, I felt at the time that all Sudanese refugees who experienced torture, trauma, and starvation in Sudan and in refugee camps deserved the right to be resettled in the Western world to put together the scattered pieces of their lives. But unfortunately, it turned out that those who could read, write and speak in English, those who had a voice and were able to verbally express themselves and articulate their needs, including some rich Ugandans, were resettled in the

Western world as South Sudanese refugees, leaving the real South Sudanese refugees, who experienced torture, trauma, lack of shelter, lack of medication, lack of education, and starvation during the Sudan civil war to suffer in Kyangwali refugee camp.

The Ugandan government's humanitarian policy allowed any person who claimed to be a refugee in Uganda to receive refugee status and benefits without careful assessment and analysis. I understand that government authorities both in Uganda and in the Western world can't do anything immediately or at all if dishonest people choose to defraud and manipulate the refugee system. All I can say it that it is not fair that some rich Ugandans have been resettled in the Western world as South Sudanese refugees when the real South Sudanese refugees are starving in Kyangwali refugee camp.

Disgracefully, some South Sudanese people who had already settled in Uganda since the Sudan first and second Anyanya wars in South Sudan, and had become Ugandan citizens, were also granted refugee status in Uganda; some of them were also resettled in the Western world, simply because they had a voice and were able to express themselves, and could afford the process. These are South Sudanese Ugandan citizens who already had food, shelter, education, medication, and some of them even had good jobs in Uganda.

A lot of the South Sudanese refugees in Kyangwali refugee camp came from Yei, Juba, Khartoum, Nimule, and a few from Kajo-Keji. There were also a few Dinka and a large number of Nuer people in Kyangwali refugee camp. Those refugees with a certain level of education and who were able to read, write and speak in English became volunteers and interpreters in the camp, helping refugees who were not able to read, write, or speak in English with completing immigration application forms.

Unfortunately, some of the untrustworthy interpreters put the wrong information on the application forms, and they instead used those people's original stories to help themselves resettle in the Western world. They succeeded, and were resettled in the Western world, leaving the owners of the stories to rot in the refugee camp. Others were unlucky because they failed their resettlement interviews. I think that the refugees who deserved to be resettled in the Western world as a matter of priority from Kyangwali refugee camp were those who were ex-soldiers (SPLA) and the wives and families of current or ex-SPLA soldiers, because their lives were in greater danger. Any refugee camp in Uganda was not a safe place for them, because the SPLA in South Sudan were able to access the refugee camps in Uganda. Unfortunately, some of these South Sudanese refugees whose lives are at greater risk still flood the substandard refugee camps in Uganda and in Kenya, and some of them have returned to their countries of origin to die there.

Whereas other South Sudanese refugee women chose to be resettled in Kyangwali refugee camp without their husbands in order to be granted quick refugee status in the Western world, other South Sudanese refugee women were genuine single mothers in the refugee camp who had lost their husbands during the Sudan civil war. These single mothers also require urgent attention and resettlement in the Western world, to enable them to put together the scattered pieces of their lives and to give their children a future. But to date, some of these vulnerable South Sudanese refugee women are still living in refugee camps in Africa and are being cut off from the world due to the language barrier.

Apart from the bad things that happened in Kyangwali refugee camp, which I have described above, this was the only refugee camp I had lived in that had community services, and there was also a social worker in the block where I lived. Being a young single woman, I was lucky enough to secure a nice home of two grass-thatched houses through the support of the social worker in the camp. This was a home of another South Sudanese refugee family (a Nuer family) who had already been resettled in the Western world. I called myself lucky at the time because, for the first time in my life, I had a house to myself and a bed, and I did things my way without anybody telling me how to live or how not to live my life. For the first time, there was no negativity around me. How beautiful is this, I thought; from sleeping on the couch in Kampala to sleeping on a nice bed in my own room. Surely miracles do happen!

Like Ibakwe refugee camp, Kyangwali refugee camp had very heavy rains throughout the year, associated with floods and lots of mud. The camp was also green, with very fertile soil. Many refugees cultivated small pieces of land, and harvested big produce each year. The most common crops grown in Kyangwali refugee camp included groundnuts, beans, maize, sweet potatoes, cabbage, onions, okra, tomatoes, and other vegetables. I also got to grow my own food, which was great. I was employed at the time so I was able to pay some people to cultivate my garden and plant some crops for me. I also paid some people to fetch for me water. As I describe below, I had three jobs while I was at Kyangwali.

I had six twenty-litre jerrycans to collect and store water for my bath, for washing my dishes and clothes, for cooking, and for drinking. Although there was a big harvest throughout the year, there hardly was any money for most refugees who were not employed in the camp. What most unemployed refugees, especially women, did was to take some of their produce and sell it to Ugandan citizens in an isolated town. Although this seemed to be the only option for some refugees to get money in the camp, getting to the town to sell the produce posed serious risks, as there was only one way to get to the town and this was through a large mountain. The women walked to the town carrying goods on their heads and on their backs, through the mountain to the town. Unfortunately, some unlucky refugees perished in the mountain on their way to the town and never returned to the camp.

This was a hard thing to deal with, but some of the refugees had no choice than to trade their produce for fish, meat, and money for other things. For some lucky refugees in Kyangwali refugee camp, including me, money was not an issue at the time, as we were employed and were paid in time. Although very little, the salary was enough to survive on, as everything was very cheap in the camp. However, transport to Hoima and to Kampala city was very expensive. One could use a whole month's salary on a day trip to Hoima or Kampala. Kyangwali refugee camp was a town-like camp, as there were many restaurants around, and there was a big central market in the camp and big occasional or holiday markets.

Compared to Oliji and Ibakwe refugee camps, Kyangwali had more than one primary school in the camp; there was also a secondary school and a school for adult learning. There was a women's group in the camp. The women were involved in making arts and crafts, and they attended quarterly meetings to talk about women's issues in the camp. There was a proper, well-equipped medical centre close to the camp; this meant that getting treatment was no longer an issue if one was sick. There was more than one borehole in the refugee camp. Clean drinking water was not a problem as it was in Oliji refugee camp.

Some refugees in Kyangwali used the history of the camp as an opportunity to turn against fellow refugees, in order to be resettled in the Western world faster. Those refugees whose background history was not strong enough to qualify them for resettlement in the Western world, especially those who came straight from big cities to the refugee camp, created problems, conflict, and enmity against other refugees through making false allegations and engaging in violent acts, especially against those refugees with no English skills and the most vulnerable, like me.

This group of Sudanese refugees did not have a story of their own to tell to qualify them for resettlement in the Western world, because they did not experience sleeping in the bush for days without food. But because they were able to express themselves verbally and in writing, they made allegations against other refugees; they told the Ugandan authorities and the UNHCR officials in the refugee camp that people did not like them in the camp because of their previous history. They demanded that they be resettled outside Africa before they were killed or before they killed themselves due to stress. Some of these refugees got away with fraud, leaving the Sudanese refugees who experienced torture and trauma as a result of the civil war suffering in the camp. Some of the refugees who used this method succeeded and were processed quickly, and resettled in the Western world before the rest of the refugees. I called this survival of the smartest.

I became a primary school teacher and a community peace education teacher, as well as an adult learning teacher. I applied for a secondary school teaching job, and I was successful, but because the secondary school was far from where I lived, and because there was no means of transport to take me there, I was instead offered a job in a school near my house, called Kasonga Primary School. One of my friends who applied for the primary school job was given my secondary school job, and I was given his primary school job. Even though I was given the primary school job, I was paid a higher salary for a primary school teacher in the camp. If I had been given the secondary school job, I would not have been able to go there at all because of my mobility difficulty, as it was far away, and worst of all, the heavy rains and the huge muddy roads in the camp made walking very difficult even for people with no mobility issues.

I didn't enjoy being a primary school teacher much, because I was assigned to teach Year One and Year Seven classes in the camp. The Year One students were very noisy and tiring. There were more than one hundred kids in the class, and there were two permanent teachers in the class (me and a Congolese male teacher). Most of the Year Seven students were older than me, and were scary and intimidating. Some of them were already married, with children in the camp. I was assigned to teach these two particular classes because the head of the school had confidence in me. He believed that I was capable of handling the pressure imposed on teachers by these two classes, because of my social work background.

I was also employed by the Department for Health in Kyangwali refugee camp on a casual basis as a community support worker for Action Against Hunger, where I became involved in administrative support in the mobilisation and immunisation of hundreds of thousands of refugee children against measles in Kyangwali refugee camp.

I, too, became a victim of conflict and enmity, physical and verbal attacks in the camp, spurred by jealousy and by people wanting to be resettled in the Western world before me. I became friends with two South Sudanese refugee families whom I met at Church in the camp. One family was from the Kuku tribe, and one family was from the Muru tribe. These two families at first treated me like one of their family members, but they later made false allegations against me, and they tried to steal my story so that they could be resettled in the Western world instead of me. Unfortunately, they were too late, because I had already told my story to the refugee officials in the camp and also to the police in the camp. They were quickly identified to be telling my story and were charged. They were caught for making other false allegations against me and against other refugees in the camp and for telling lies to be granted refugee status.

One of the families was later deported to South Sudan for manipulating the refugee system for their own gain, and was refused entry to Uganda, or any other country for that matter. The woman claimed that her husband died in the war, but her husband was actually well and alive in South Sudan. He was one of the rich SPLA in South Sudan. This woman alleged that I threatened to kill her and her six children. She was in her forties and I was in my twenties. She was six foot seven tall, and I was four foot two. Now I am 5 foot 4 tall. She weight over seventy kilos, and I weighed forty-three kilos. I was so small, with a physical disability, but she claimed that she was scared of me because I was going to go to her house in the night and set her house on fire when they were sleeping. She lived about one hour away from where I lived, but she claimed that I was going to kill her and her children, when I have great mobility difficulties!

The police laughed at her claims and she walked away with a serious warning from the police and embarrassment. The police called her "insane". The second family also made similar allegations about me, and they said that they too were scared of me. This family had mum, dad, and four children, but they claimed that they were scared of me! The two families asked the police and the UNHCR authorities in the camp to remove me from the camp because I was a "threat" to their lives and families. These two families were friends with each other, and threatened to harm me physically and set my house on fire. The threats were made on separate occasions.

They were jealous that their older children, who were older than me, were not working like I was. They hated the fact that I was given a good home, and that I was working as a school teacher in one of the primary schools, and I was earning money while they were unemployed. The police responded by issuing them with a restraining order, which stated that they were not to come to my home, and if they were to see me in the market or anywhere, they should walk away. If they talked to me or approached me in any way, they would be arrested and deported. The police also provided security in my home for a period of time to ensure that I was safe. The UNHCR office in the camp responded by offering me a possible resettlement in the United Kingdom (UK).

Twelve

Coming to Australia as a Refugee

In my application for resettlement in the UK, I was screened for an initial interview, which was successful, and my name appeared on the list of those refugees who were to be resettled in the UK. I told my sister in Australia that I had been screened to go to the UK, but my sister told me not to do the next set of interviews, which were to be followed with a medical examination, a visa, and resettlement in the UK. She instead suggested that I leave Kyangwali refugee camp immediately, go to Ibakwe refugee camp, collect my mother, go to Kampala, and wait for her to contact me with Australian visa application forms. My sister didn't want me to leave my mother in Ibakwe refugee camp by herself.

That's why I applied to be resettled in Australia, and I came to Australia with my mother instead. I left

Kyangwali refugee camp in the night without any of the refugees knowing. Only the police and the UNCHR office in the camp knew of my trip to Kampala. The UNHCR office said that I could still process to go to the UK from Kampala city if I had a place to stay and a phone that they could ring me on to communicate with me in relation to my UK resettlement process. But my process to Australia was quick and successful, so I came to Australia instead. And I am happy that I am in Australia. I don't know what life would have been like for me if I had gone to the UK.

I believe that the reason why I was targeted in Kyangwali refugee camp was because of my level of education, and because I was the youngest refugee woman with a disability ever employed in the refugee camp. I also worked as a Church secretary in a Pentecostal Church in the camp, and I was an adult education teacher teaching older people to read, write and speak in English. I went to Kyangwali refugee camp after completing my Social Work Diploma in Kampala, Uganda. It was unusual at the time for young South Sudanese women like me to obtain higher education levels, let alone women with disabilities.

The South Sudanese refugees who were resettled in Australia came with nothing, and they had to start from zero in Australia. People like me who didn't have birth certificates guessed our ages. Because the South Sudanese refugees lost everything during the Sudan civil war, a lot of the South Sudanese refugees who were in their sixties and seventies were resettled in Australia as people in their forties and fifties, and those in their forties and fifties were resettled in Australia as people in their thirties and twenties. This meant that those South Sudanese Australians who were over sixty years old, and should have been considered as seniors and received the age pension, were required by Centrelink to look for full time paid jobs. Those who should have had breast and bowel cancer screening at fifty years of age in Australia missed out on that screening because they were unable to prove their real age to authorities in Australia. Refugees were told in Uganda that if they say that they were over fifty years old, their visa application may not be successful and that the Australian government may consider them as a liability to Australia instead of being an asset. This is the reason why the South Sudanese refugees had to reduce their age to be accepted to enter and live in Australia. This explains the reasons why the majority of the South Sudanese Australians have their birthdays on the first of January.

It was hard for people like me who didn't have birth certificates to change my age to a more realistic one in Australia. I know that I am younger than the age stated in my Australian visa. I had to increase my age by a few years to enable me to be the main applicant on my visa application form. If I didn't increase my age, then my mother, who didn't speak English, would have been the main applicant, and she would have been the person to answer the questions during the interview with the help of an interpreter, and interpreters were highly untrustworthy at the time. A good number of the South Sudanese refugees failed their interview, and were not able to resettle in Australia, because their interpreters didn't interpret the information to the Australian interviewers correctly.

Those South Sudanese refugees who lost their certificates of education and their higher educational qualifications during the Sudan civil war had to start from zero level in Australia. Many South Sudanese refugees' documents, including birth certificates and educational qualifications, were destroyed, burnt, or lost during the war. Some of the South Sudanese refugees were doctors, engineers, and teachers back in South Sudan, but here in Australia, they have to do the work of a cleaner, carer/support worker, or work in a factory and study at the same time to obtain Australian educational qualifications that will enable them to secure an office job in Australia. Their qualifications from South Sudan, Uganda and Kenya are not considered to be good enough to enable them enter into university in Australia or to enable them secure an office job in Australia. Their qualifications have to be assessed as soon as they arrive in Australia, and they have to attend 850 hours of training in English as part of their resettlement requirement. In South Australia, for example, they also attend a bridging course before they can be granted entry to the university.

Can you imagine working in Sudan as a doctor, a surgeon, an engineer, a nurse, a school principal, or the head of a hospital, for example, then coming to Australia and working as a cleaner scrubbing toilets, and then going to college or university all over again? Can you imagine the feeling of worthlessness that South Sudanese people may suffer in Australia? How do you go home at the end of the day, as a man, a husband, and a father, and tell your wife and children that you have been scrubbing toilets all day to earn a living? How do you tell your family, relatives and friends back home that your current job now is to clean offices and scrub toilets, when you were the most highly honoured and respected member of your community back in South Sudan?

After fleeing South Sudan, I endured a harsh life and violations of human rights as a refugee in three different refugee camps in Uganda for nineteen years.

I had been exposed to an unsafe and unhygienic living environment, lack of food, lack of clean water and lack of shelter. I applied to come to Australia as a refugee in April 2004, and in April 2005, my application was approved. My sister, Angelina, who was already in Australia at the time, proposed for me to come to Australia, and I was granted a Humanitarian Visa.

I came to Australia with my mother. She went back to South Sudan to visit family in 2012, but she became sick and passed away in May 2016. She was planning to return to Australia when she died. She died two days before my youngest daughter was born. I was hopeful that when I arrived in Australia, I could apply for my sister Selina in Uganda and perhaps my brother James in South Sudan to join me in Australia. Unfortunately, after arriving Australia, I discovered that I couldn't bring my sister or brother to Australia with the government's help, because they were in different countries. My brother is considered to be the last family member left in South Sudan, and my sister is considered to be the last family member left in Uganda. For them to come to Australia, I will have to bring them privately and look after them in Australia for two years before they can receive any government assistance. My sister has four children and my brother has seven children. Those are two big families for me and Angelina to look after without any government assistance.

My resettlement in Australia has given me new hope for the future, because I have been able to put together the scattered pieces of my life, and I am now a happy mother of two beautiful daughters aged eight and two and a half. I have a Bachelors degree in Social Work, and a Masters degree in Mediation and Conflict Resolution from the University of South Australia. I worked with Families SA and with the Child Abuse Report Line in South Australia as a Social Worker from December 2007 to June 2009, as well as working with Disability SA as a Social Worker, Service Coordinator, Intake Coordinator, Case Manager, and a Facilitator for the Individualised Funding Team from August 2009 to July 2013. I have recently worked with the Young Women's Christian Association Adelaide (YWCA) as a Coordinator for the Crossing the Bridge Project, which aims to support African women with disabilities in South Australia. I was the founder of the Crossing the Bridge Project. In 2014, I ran for parliament as a lead candidate in the Upper House with the Dignity for Disability Party, and I also ran for parliament with the Dignity Party South Australia as a number four on the Upper House ticket for the South Australian 2018 State Election, supporting the Honourable Kelly Vincent, and representing people with disabilities in the South

Australian community in the area of education, public housing, employment, access and social justices. The Dignity Party is a small South Australian-based political party that represents people with disabilities in South Australia.

Because of the hardships I experienced in my childhood, I reckon I should have done one thing after arriving in Australia—lain down on the couch and slept and watched TV all day, and eaten a lot of food every day, to make up for the years I spent hungry in my childhood and in the refugee camps. You could say that I have a lot of reasons not to get out of bed every morning, not only because of my past, but because of my disability and the pain and fatigue I experience on a daily basis as a result of my post-polio syndrome.

But instead, I chose to go to university, and then to work. I am not working at present because I have two little daughters to look after. I am a stay-home mum and an author. I look forward to getting back into the workforce once my younger daughter starts school. Because I believe that disability is not inability, I chose to go to university and then to work, and I have learnt to drive a car. I got my driver's licence within two years of arriving in Australia, and it makes getting around so much easier.

Before I got my driver's licence, and before I was

provided with an electric wheelchair to aid my mobility outside of the house and to enable me to access my community and the University campus, I had great difficulty using public transport and getting out into the community, and as a result, I became housebound, especially on weekends and public holidays. Getting around the university campus was also a challenge, but the wheelchair provided by Disability SA and by the University of South Australia, Magill Campus, made things a lot easier for me, and I am now more independent. I used to walk to the bus stop in the rain, in the cold, in the heat, and in the dark to catch a bus to the University, but all that changed after I got my driver's licence.

Thirteen
Transport

Many refugee women who were used to walking everywhere in their countries of origin experience difficulties in accessing public transport here in Australia, due to language barriers and a lack of awareness about what bus to catch, where to catch the bus from, and where to buy bus tickets from. As a result, they become isolated and housebound here in Australia. Many of them have gained excessive weight within a few years of being in Australia due to lack of exercise, resulting in many health issues. The language barrier also means that these refugee women buy very cheap unhealthy food, which may not be good for their health, as they don't know how to read food labels. Others who experience domestic violence have no money to purchase bus tickets.

When I first came to Australia, I too didn't know

what bus number to catch to the city and back to where I was staying, and where to buy bus tickets from. I didn't know which way to stand and where to catch the bus from if I was going to the city, but the Australian Refugee Association of South Australia (ARA) helped me resettle in Australia. They linked me with a social worker who taught me how to access the services. They linked me with a friend, someone I could ring at any time if I needed help with anything, or if I just wanted to talk. They linked me with someone to help me with homework; (An Aboriginal lady) that woman helped me complete my university application forms, and she also linked me with other services. She helped me with transport and took me to appointments, such as Centrelink pension eligibility appointments.

I attended a number of assessments with Centrelink where medical reports were provided, and I was granted the Disability Support Pension. ARA referred me to the Migrant Health Services for an initial health check. The Migrant Health Services then referred me to the Royal Adelaide Hospital. It was at the Royal Adelaide Hospital that I was diagnosed with post-polio syndrome. The Royal Adelaide Hospital then referred me to the polio specialists at the Queen Elizabeth Hospital for polio specialist services. ARA helped me with paying my first bills, and they referred me to a financial counsellor with Families SA to enable me manage my finances well and to pay rent, bills and buy food. ARA sent me to the Salvation Army for more financial and food support until I was settled. ARA helped me with my first furniture and with moving house. ARA linked me with Disability Rights Advocacy Services Inc (formerly known as MALSSA) for Disability Advocacy Services.

MALSSA was the Service that helped me access legal services following the sudden termination of my employment with Families SA (see Chapter Fifteen). ARA linked me with Disability SA for in-home and community support services. ARA helped me attend my first orientation information sessions in 2005 with the police, the cancer council of South Australia, with Centrelink, and with other service providers, to help me understand the Australian law, how to keep myself safe from strangers and from sunburn, and how and where to access services. ARA also helped me with food until I was settled in Australia. My sister helped me open a bank account and register with Centrelink and Medicare. She was also the one that took me to ARA for the first time.

Fourteen
Education

I am glad to say that I came to Australia when I already knew how to read, write and speak in English. Nevertheless, I still had to attend 850 hours of English classes in South Australia in 2005 and in early 2006 as part of my resettlement requirement. What I struggled with at first was the Australian accent, but through listening to the radio and watching TV, I was able to understand the Australian way of speaking. Even though I still have a little bit of Ugandan accent left, I am now able to speak with an Australian accent.

My Diploma in Social Work helped me to apply to the university in South Australia. After arriving in Australia, I started asking for help in my community about going to the university, but all I got was negative advice. People told me that I would never get in to the university because I only had a diploma. They said that my diploma would not be recognised. They explained that many people came to Australia with PhDs from South Sudan, but their qualifications were not recognised, and they had to start from zero. Others advised me to join a Technical and Further Education Institute (TAFE) to complete a course, and then do a bridging course that would enable me to join the university in South Australia if I was lucky. I had even enrolled to do a TAFE course, but deep in my heart, I knew that I had to go to the university directly without going to TAFE.

I said to myself, I am going to do things my way, without the support of my community, and I will go to the university. I spoke to my English teacher, who provided me with a contact number for the University of South Australia — Magill Campus. She told me to ring the number and ask to speak to Frank, who was the head of the Social Work Department at Magill campus at the time. I rang the number and I spoke to Frank, and he gave me a time to go and see him in Magill. Frank told me that my diploma was acceptable, given it was from Uganda. He told me to apply through the South Australian Tertiary Admission Centre (SATAC), and he said that if SATAC asked me to go and sit for an

English Test, I should tell them that I had already done the English test at Magill Campus, and I should give them his number.

Frank not only accepted me at the university to complete my social work degree, but he also gave me two years' credit. So I started my Social Work degree studies here in Adelaide from third year! A few weeks later, a letter was in my letterbox advising me that I had been admitted to the University of South Australia to complete my social work degree. There was a letter and a form included with my admission letter, asking me to go and sit an English test for my admission to be completed. I rang them and told them that I had already done an assessment at Magill campus, and I asked them to ring Frank. I ended the call and rang Frank to tell him that I had received my admission letter. A few minutes later, Frank rang me to advise that he has spoken to SATAC, who would contact me soon about completing my university admission process. About an hour later, I received a call from SATAC advising me that I no longer needed to sit a test in English. The woman I spoke to said that I should go ahead with completing my other admission requirements and I would be free to join the university.

I was blown away. I thought I was dreaming. I pinched myself and I rubbed my eyes to wake myself up, but I was wide-awake. I said to myself, if I had listened to the negativity around me, I would not have joined the university in South Australia. I was fortunate enough to enrol at the university and complete my bachelors' degree and masters' degree studies with limited assistance because of my determination in life. I was also fortunate enough to be given the opportunity to use the University's distant library services, where every book I borrowed was delivered to my home as a matter of priority, and then returned to the university once I have finished reading the books. All these happened because I am very articulate in addressing my needs. Not every refugee woman with a disability is able to speak for herself, and may function better through the help of an advocate. I have, however, required extra time to complete my assignments because of the pain and fatigue that I experience on a daily basis.

Fifteen
Employment Challenges

After arriving in Australia, I said, hooray, I am in a free country! Now I can put back together the scattered pieces of my life, settle down, and have a family. I thought that I had left all the hardships behind in the refugee camps, and now I could focus on going to University, getting a job, settling down, getting married and having a family.

What I didn't know was that there were still challenges for me to face and overcome in Australia to achieve my goals of study, employment, and relationships. Before my employment with Families SA was terminated in June 2009, my team had organised a team lunch which I was not informed of. One beautiful afternoon, I was left in the office all by myself, wondering where my team had gone. I found out later that they had gone out to lunch without me. A week later, I was ambushed by the Families SA manager and confronted with some allegations made by my supervisor, and I was sacked on the spot. I was not given any opportunity to respond to the allegations, but sacked without pay before I was proven guilty. I was only given five minutes to clear my desk and leave the office immediately, which I did.

I found out a few minutes after I left the office that the manager had circulated an email advising staff that I had decided to leave work before the end of my contract for personal reasons, and that staff should respect my privacy and not contact or approach me in any way. One of my friends from the office rang me, asking if everything was all right with me. He told me about the content of the email from the manager. He forwarded the email to his private email, and printed a copy out for me. Two days before I was sacked, I had been offered a permanent job with Housing SA, and my Families SA supervisor was aware of it. Because my Families SA manager was determined not to let me sign the contract to get the permanent job, she contacted the Housing SA manager and told her that I was under investigation with Families SA for misconduct. The Housing SA manager then contacted me to inform me that she had decided to withdraw the job offer, because their policy prevented them from employing people who were under investigation by another employer for misconduct. When I later launched a complaint with the department's Human Resources office, I was shocked to discover that my manager had advised Human Resources that I had resigned before the end of my contract for personal reasons, and therefore, I was not entitled to any payment. The Human Resources office told me that there was nothing written in the system to suggest that I was under investigation for misconduct. They said that all investigations went through them, and that no manager in their department had the power to recommend any staff investigation without a disciplinary hearing organised by the Human Resources department.

I sought legal advice from a migration lawyer in Adelaide, and we started legal proceedings. We were going to ask that Families SA pay me for the loss of my Housing SA employment until retirement age, which was sixty-five years in South Australia if the case was settled before 2015, otherwise it would be seventy-two years retirement age. After three meetings with the lawyer, the industrial law court and the CEO of Families SA, I was offered a six months contract with Disability SA, with a possibility of renewing the contract. The lawyer advised me to take the job, so I did, and I worked with Disability SA for five years. After I signed the contract with Disability SA, my lawyer dropped the case. Disability SA, Families SA and Housing SA were all under the same Department at the time (Department for Families and Communities). My lawyer said that if I refused to take the job, they would argue that I was offered another job but I refused it, and I might end up losing the case and walking away with nothing. We were seeking compensation for defamation and losses.

I was not paid the annual leave that I was entitled to, and I ended up losing a permanent job with Housing SA that would have made a big difference in my life and in my family's life. I think that the reasons I was targeted were my disability, my refugee background, English being my second language, and being a single mother. Sometimes I wonder if that lunch was organised to discuss my sacking, and that's why I was not invited. I also think that I was targeted because I was the one chosen to represent the department at an International African Women's Conference hosted by Flinders University in South Australia, in October 2012. I gave a speech at this conference about the challenges faced by African people with disabilities in Australia. I was the keynote speaker at this conference. I was also invited by the Special Investigation Unit (SIU) in April 2009 to give a speech to the SIU Board members about appropriate ways of working with refugees and survivors of torture and trauma, following a tragic stabbing of a South Sudanese boy in Adelaide City. I received excellent feedback from Flinders University and from the SIU through my Families SA and Disability SA manager after my speech; but they weren't happy about it. They said that they have worked with the department for many years, and none of them had ever been invited to give a speech anywhere.

In January 2013, I was told by my manager in Disability SA that my contract was not going to be renewed, because they no longer had the capacity to employ staff on contract. I accepted that that was all it was, so I asked for a work report from my manager so I could apply for other jobs. I was shocked to read in the report that they could no longer employ me; apparently, I was untrainable because English was my second language. The manager said that she would re-employ me if I had further training in English. This time I knew what my rights were. I sent an email to the program manager, requesting to meet with her to discuss the work report, which I attached to the email. Three days later, I received an email from the program manager with a job offer in another Disability SA office, and I took the job. The information in my work report didn't reflect the information in my employee folder with Disability SA, which was written by the same manager. I later learnt that there was no copy of the work report given to me in my Disability SA employee folder. For the five years I had been working with Disability SA, there was nothing written in my supervision notes to suggest that I needed to improve in certain areas, especially English. Nor was I employed on a provisional basis.

It is sad to know that there are many refugees and new migrants in Australia who have experienced or are experiencing discrimination in one way or the other. Because of this, a lot of the African refugee migrants, for example, have not been able to settle in Australia, even after ten years of being here. This has resulted in ongoing mental health issues, relationship and family breakdowns, and poverty. This is unacceptable, and these issues need to be addressed.

I was also bullied at work when I was working with Families SA's Child Abuse Report Line. There was a guy who worked there who always had something to say about me—how I looked, how I walked, the food I ate, the colour of my skin, and my background. He said that it is disgraceful for Australians to employ black people like me to take their jobs and money when there are a lot of unemployed white Australians. One day, this man told me that the best job for refugee people with disabilities like me would be to go and pick up dog poo at someone's house in return for food!

I didn't do anything about his bullying, because I was still new in Australia, and shy, and I didn't know what my rights were. However, I asked him to write me a recommendation letter to enable me get the dog poo job, but he refused. If he had written that letter, I would have used it to get back at him. I was offered another job in another Families SA office a few weeks after I stopped working there, so I focused my energy on more important things.

Sixteen

Daily Living Skills and Support

I have difficulties completing day-to-day living activities such as cleaning and shopping due to the effects of the post-polio syndrome that I experience daily. For example, hanging the washing out and taking the washing back in is a very difficult and challenging task for me to complete, due to my sore feet and sore lower back. Standing while hanging clothes on the clothesline, and while chopping vegetables and cooking, as well as lifting heavy stuff, are also very difficult tasks for me to complete. However, I am very grateful for the in-home support that the Australian government has provided for me. I have support workers who come to my house twice a week and help with doing the things that I have difficulty completing. I also have a kitchen stool that I can sit on when I'm washing my dishes and cooking.

The provision of necessary home modifications also helps me to manage my independence. Providing in-home support services also enables people living with disabilities to live independently.

A lot of people, especially women with disabilities, report experiencing physical abuse, sexual abuse, financial abuse, psychological abuse, social isolation and neglect; they may also not be able to access appropriate medical treatment, and are deprived of opportunities, thus rendering them powerless and more disadvantaged than any actual experience of having a disability can make them. This abuse may be perpetrated by family members, carers, male partners who are the primary care givers, support workers, residential care workers, bus or taxi drivers, teachers or mentors, and/or medical professionals. Such abuse is, however, not spoken of, or not reported, as victims may fear losing their carers, losing financial support, or losing their wheelchair-accessible accommodation. They fear losing services; some government funding policies in South Australia, for example, state that a person with a disability must have a fulltime carer for them to be eligible for some disability-specific services in their own home and in the community.

It is important to acknowledge that people with profound intellectual disability or brain injury may not have the capacity to recognise what abuse look like, while other people with disabilities, who grew up in a culture of negativity, are able to recognise abuse, but may not report it, as they have been told all their lives that abuse is "normal", and if they report it, they may not be believed anyway. Because I have a voice and because I am able to articulate my needs, if I don't like what a support worker has done in my house, I am able to ring the service provider, report what was done wrong, and request another support worker. Unfortunately, the majority of the people living with disabilities have no voice, and others need encouragement to use their voice.

Seventeen

Language Barrier

I was lucky, because I came to Australia when I was able to speak, read and write in English, but most refugees and new migrants in Australia, with or without disabilities, have difficulty expressing themselves, and difficulties speaking the language. They experience challenges in negotiating services such as the health care system, the National Disability Insurance Scheme (NDIS), and many others. Accessing education and the health care system can be very difficult for new migrants, due to the language barrier. In addition to the language barrier, many refugee migrants with disabilities are not able to access the NDIS, because all information about the NDIS is mainly available online. If you are not computer literate, or if you do not have access to the Internet, it can be very difficult to access this information. The NDIS uses an online portal that participants can log-in to, to view the funding they have left in their plan. There have been a number of reported issues with the portal not reflecting up-to-date information, which can be confusing. If you want an update on the funding you have left, but don't use a computer, you have to call the 1800 number, which can often mean a long wait time, and can be challenging for people who don't speak or read in English or in their own language.

Confidentiality and/or privacy cannot be guaranteed where there is domestic/family violence if the only interpreter in the community is a family member, or a friend of the perpetrator. If an individual requires an interpreter to attend an appointment that is related to their disability, health or legal issues, finding a trusted interpreter can be challenging for those South Sudanese Australians, for example, who have very limited or no English skills. As a result, some South Sudanese Australians have been relying on family members to interpret at their appointments, which can pose serious confidentiality issues if they do not have a relationship of trust and safety with the person.

My advice to any refugee or new migrant in Australia, and to any person in Australia with a disability, is that if you are facing issues at work or at the university, and you don't know what to do or what your rights are because you are new in Australia, because you have a disability or because you don't know how to speak English, please don't keep quiet — speak up! Talk to someone about it, and take the necessary steps to address the issue before it pulls you down.

Whether you are in a wheelchair or on your feet, whether you have a mental illness or a medical condition, whether you are a refugee or not, whether you are a woman or a single parent, you can choose to make a difference in your community, regardless of your physical limitations and regardless of your background and status. Don't let your disability, mental illness, medical condition, age, status, sexuality, language barrier or background define you.

Let your ability define who you are, and always remember that DISABILITY IS NOT INABILITY and that age is just a number, and that being a refugee is just a name. No situation or condition is permanent. If people around you are negative towards you, use that negativity to make something positive in your life. I understand that people with disabilities, women, refugees, and others among the most vulnerable people in society have no control over what people think of them, or what people may say about them.

But if you can, stay away from negative people and surround yourself with positive thinking people. Despite all the negative things that have happened to me in Australia, I am so grateful that I am in Australia, and that I am raising my two beautiful daughters here. I do not know what life would have been like for me if I were still back in the refugee camps, and if I were raising my daughters in Africa, where there is no welfare and government support.

Although I had a childhood of extreme poverty and was exposed to violence in the refugee camps, I was a strong young girl. My determination and positive approach to life have helped me to overcome all the hardships of my childhood, and I grew into a strong young woman. My hardships made me the strong woman that I am today. In the past, people saw the disability in me but not me as a person. I hope that by reading my story in this book, people will start to see me as a person but not as a disability or a burden.

www.ingramcontent.com/pod-product-compliance
Lightning Source LLC
Chambersburg PA
CBHW031851090426
42741CB00005B/439